D1479275

Insights You Need from
**Harvard
Business
Review**

GLOBAL
RECESSION

Insights You Need from Harvard Business Review

Business is changing. Will you adapt or be left behind?

Get up to speed and deepen your understanding of the topics that are shaping your company's future with the **Insights You Need from Harvard Business Review series**. Featuring HBR's smartest thinking on fast-moving issues—blockchain, cybersecurity, AI, and more—each book provides the foundation introduction and practical case studies your organization needs to compete today and collects the best research, interviews, and analysis to get it ready for tomorrow.

You can't afford to ignore how these issues will transform the landscape of business and society. The Insights You Need series will help you grasp these critical ideas—and prepare you and your company for the future.

Books in the series includes:

Agile

Artificial Intelligence

Blockchain

Climate Change

Coronavirus: Leadership and Recovery

Customer Data and Privacy

Cybersecurity

Monopolies and Tech Giants

Racial Justice

Strategic Analytics

The Year in Tech, 2021

Insights You Need from
Harvard Business Review

GLOBAL RECESSION

Harvard Business Review Press
Boston, Massachusetts

Copyright 2021 Harvard Business School Publishing Corporation
All rights reserved
Printed in the United States of America

10 9 8 7 6 5 4 3 2 1

The web addresses referenced in this book were live and correct at the time of the book's publication but may be subject to change.

Cataloging-in-Publication data is forthcoming.

ISBN: 978-1-64782-134-0
eISBN: 978-1-64782-135-7

The paper used in this publication meets the requirements of the American National Standard for Permanence of Paper for Publications and Documents in Libraries and Archives Z39.48-1992

Contents

Contents

Section 3

Entrepreneurship and Startups in the Recession

Section 4

Managing Yourself and Your Career in the Recession

Introduction

FINDING OPPORTUNITY IN ADVERSITY

by Martin Reeves

Most business leaders have little experience to draw on when managing their company through a recession. Even those with the longest tenures have only faced a handful of major shocks, each with different causes and effects (just think about the contrasting dynamics of the Great Recession and Covid-19). Lacking experience, they often fall back on intuition to guide their behavior. Unfortunately, evidence from past recessions shows that these apparently reasonable intuitions are often misleading and sometimes severely damaging. Four of these mistaken ideas crop up most commonly.

First, leaders often see recessions as temporary deviations from their company's long-term competitive game, so they set their strategic goals aside in favor of three short-term ones: survive, ameliorate damage, and prepare to get back to business as usual when growth resumes. In reality, recessions should not be considered a break from long-run competitive trends—what happens during crises actually has a *disproportionate* effect on long-term success. Our analysis shows that although crises (defined as quarters in which an industry's total shareholder return declines by at least 15 percent) occur only about 10 percent of quarters, they account for more than 30 percent of long-run outperformance. In fact, two-thirds of companies that sustain long-term high performance also outperform during crises.

Next there is the intuition that all companies need to prepare for lower performance during a crisis. Lowering expectations in this way can become a self-fulfilling prophesy. Our research shows that one in seven companies *increased* both top-line and bottom-line performance in absolute terms during the last four U.S. economic downturns.

A related common belief is that what sector you are in largely determines performance in a crisis. This can lead to complacency or fatalism. In fact, a significant share of companies flourishes in every sector during crises, even ones considered as highly cyclical. Sector is not fate.

Finally, crisis strategy tends to focus on operational discipline and cost management above all else. This is understandable since cash-flow viability is a minimum condition for survival in harsh times. But the evidence is clear on where the competitive gains of superior crisis performance accrue. Growth and the expectations of future growth are the dominant drivers of outperformance in downturns.

While deep crises are rare, deviations from plans and trends are becoming more the norm than the exception. With rising turbulence driven by technological, economic, political, and social shocks, avoiding the traps of these four mistakes is imperative. Across all industries, today's market leaders lose their performance edge and fade back to average much faster than before. To succeed in the long term, we now need to build "all-weather companies"—businesses that don't merely survive crises but emerge from them in better shape than they started.

Leaders therefore need to design their companies not for optimality in good times but rather for resilience in the face of unpredictable shifts in the business environment. Resilience represents the capacity for organizations to resist or absorb shocks, recover from them, and thrive in new circumstances. This requires a broader tool kit than traditional risk management, which deals with insuring against specific risks that have known distributions. Companies now must be able to withstand a wide range of potential events, many of which may be fundamentally unknowable until they occur. And they must build resilient capabilities preemptively because by the time a shock hits it may be too late.

Companies must also be able to adapt and reinvent their offerings and business models because upheavals often have lasting effects on consumer behavior and societal beliefs—providing new opportunities for those who act on them quickest. Just as World War II propelled the development and commercialization of a series of inventions that shaped the postwar era, including rocketry, jet engines, pressurized aircraft cabins, the helicopter, artificial rubber, penicillin, radar, and more, the Covid-19 crisis will likely be looked back on as giving birth to new needs, products, and services and accelerating the growth of the resilience of companies that exploited them.

These imperatives to preemptively build resilience to unfavorable events and taking bold action to capitalize on new opportunities when a crisis hits run throughout this collection. By bringing together perspectives across a range of related topics, *HBR* has provided a great resource for leaders to understand how to win in recessions.

As Ranjay Gulati and Mark Wiedman write in their contribution, many firms struggle to respond quickly and proactively when crises arise, but those that redirect resources toward new opportunities are the most likely to succeed.

The first two sections of this collection, "Strategy in the Recession" and "Managing Your Business Through the Recession," cover a number of considerations across different parts of the business. It discusses how leaders should reconsider their partnerships, strategies, supply chains, sales channels, and marketing activities during downturns as well as ways to rethink how they allocate resources, reorganize companies, and seek new opportunities when a crisis strikes.

Next, the "Entrepreneurship and Startups in the Recession" section discusses challenges faced by new or prospective businesses during a downturn. While the conventional wisdom may be that downturns are a challenging time to start or grow a new business, these contributors show that there is ample opportunity to succeed, even when the circumstances seem especially harsh.

The final section, "Managing Yourself and Your Career in the Recession," turns to the personal side of business. It offers tips for those who have been unlucky enough to be laid off during a crisis and examines how everyone can use an unfavorable event to spark personal growth.

Paradoxically, crises are also a time for optimism—they bring not only elevated risks but also elevated opportunities. This collection will help forward-looking leaders aspire to design companies capable of emerging from a crisis stronger.

Section 1

STRATEGY IN THE RECESSION

1

ADAPT YOUR BUSINESS TO THE NEW REALITY

by Michael G. Jacobides and Martin Reeves

I t will be quite some time before we understand the full impact of the Covid-19 pandemic. But the history of such shocks tells us two things. First, even in severe economic downturns and recessions, some companies are able to gain advantage. Among large firms doing business during the past four downturns, 14 percent increased both sales growth rate and EBIT margin.

Second, crises produce not just a plethora of temporary changes (mainly short-term shifts in demand) but also some lasting ones. For example, the 9/11 terrorist attacks caused only a temporary decline in air travel, but they brought about a lasting shift in societal attitudes about the trade-off between privacy and security, resulting in permanently higher levels of screening and surveillance. Similarly, the 2003 SARS outbreak in China is often credited with accelerating a structural shift to e-commerce, paving the way for the rise of Alibaba and other digital giants.

In the following pages we'll discuss how companies can reassess their growth opportunities in the new normal, reconfigure their business models to better realize those opportunities, and reallocate their capital more effectively.

Reassess Growth Opportunities

The Covid-19 pandemic has severely disrupted global consumption, forcing (and permitting) people to unlearn old habits and adopt new ones. A study on habit formation suggests that the average time for a new habit to form is 66 days, with a minimum of 21 days. As of this writing, the lockdown has already lasted long enough in many countries to significantly change habits that had been the foundation of demand and supply.

Companies seeking to emerge from the crisis in a stronger position must develop a systematic understanding of changing habits. For many firms, that will require a new process for detecting and assessing shifts before they become obvious to all. The first step is to map the potential ramifications of behavioral trends to identify specific products or business opportunities that will most likely grow or contract as a result (see figure 1-1). Consider how the pandemic has caused people to stay at home more. Implications include an increase in home office refurbishment, driving greater demand for products ranging from paint to printers. Unless we sensitize ourselves to new habits and their cascading indirect effects, we will fail to spot weak signals and miss opportunities to shape markets.

The next step is to categorize demand shifts using a simple 2×2 matrix, on the basis of whether they are likely to be short-term or long-term and whether they were existing trends before the crisis or have emerged since it began (see figure 1-2). The four quadrants distinguish among boosts (temporary departures from existing trends), displacements (temporary new trends), catalysts (accelerations of existing trends), and innovations (new lasting trends). Consider again the behavioral shift of "stay at home more," which has had a serious impact on retail shopping. The question is, Will the shift away from retail stores to online be temporary, or will it be a structural

FIGURE 1-1

Step 1: Cascade changes in habit

Start by drilling down from a big behavioral shift to identify specific products or business opportunities that are likely to grow or contract as the result of the pandemic.

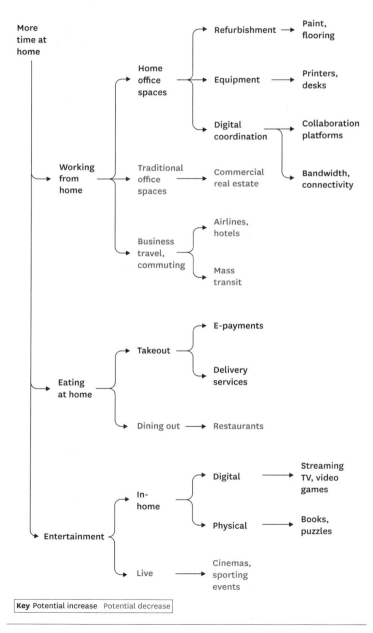

FIGURE 1-2

Step 2: Identify type and duration of new trends

Categorize behavioral shifts according to whether they are likely to be short- or long-term and whether they existed before the pandemic or are new since it began. Entertainment, for instance, shows opportunity in each of the four quadrants.

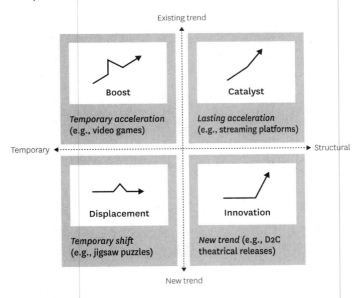

Source: BCG Henderson Institute.

change with permanent knock-on effects in other areas, such as commercial real estate?

We would place shopping in the catalyst quadrant. The pandemic has amplified and accelerated an existing trend rather than created a new one; people were shifting to e-shopping before the lockdown. But the shift is

7

structural rather than temporary because the scale and duration of the enforced switch, coupled with the generally positive performance of the channel, suggests that in many shopping categories customers will see no need to switch back. So, retailers must shape their strategies to the new normal. Indeed, before the lockdown many retailers were responding to the digital challenge by redefining the purpose of the physical store, often by reimagining shopping as not a chore but an attractive social experience.

This framework can therefore be used to highlight which trends to follow and which to shape more aggressively. Companies cannot pursue all possibilities and should not try to. To get an idea of which ones to back, ask yourself whether any shift in demand is temporary or permanent. Many of the immediately observed shifts in response to Covid-19 were driven by fear of infection or compliance with official directives and therefore were most likely temporary. But others were accompanied by greater convenience or better economics, so they are more likely to stick.

Any analysis of growth opportunities must go well beyond a simple categorization of what you already know. You need to challenge your ideas about what's happening in your traditional business domains by taking a fresh, careful look at the data. This requires that you actively seek out anomalies and surprises.

Dive deep into the data.

Anomalies usually emerge from data that is both granular (revealing patterns hidden by top-line averages) and high-frequency (allowing emerging patterns to be identified rapidly). As behavior changed with the outbreak of Covid-19, for example, rich sources included data on foot traffic and credit card spending. An analysis showed that the recent drop-off in cinema attendance occurred before theaters were shut down in the United States. This, combined with an existing trend of declining attendance, suggested that the shift was consumer-driven and perhaps likely to persist in the absence of innovation. Live sports attendance, in contrast, declined only when events were officially canceled, suggesting a stronger possibility of a behavioral rebound.

Take multiple perspectives.

In the military, a technique for discovering what you don't know is to use the "eyes of the enemy." Military leaders ask themselves, What is the enemy paying attention to? and then shift their own attention accordingly to illuminate potential blind spots and alternative perspectives.

The same can be applied to industry mavericks and competitors: Who is doing well? What market segments are your rivals focused on? What products or services are they launching? The same principle can be extended to customers: Which ones are exhibiting new behaviors? Which have stayed loyal? What new crisis-induced needs do customers have, and what are they paying attention to? It can even be applied to countries: What patterns emerged in China, where both the outbreak and the recovery came ahead of those in Western nations? In your own organization, ask: Which workplace innovations are taking hold in leading firms? What new needs are employees responding to? What opportunities do they represent that could potentially be developed and rolled out more broadly?

Armed with an understanding of where your opportunities lie, you can now move to the next step: shaping your business model to capture them.

Reconfigure Your Business Model

Your new business model will be shaped by the demand and supply shifts relevant to your industry. Many manufacturing companies, for example, will be profoundly affected by the structural and likely permanent shocks to globalization brought on by the pandemic. With big markets such as the United States raising trade barriers, for example, many companies will need to reshore critical components in their supply chains—from R&D down to assembly.

To figure out what business model the new normal requires, you need to ask basic questions about how you create and deliver value, who you'll partner with, and who your customers will be. As an example, let's look at how retail shopping businesses should be adjusting to the demand shift to digital.

Can you take the value you offer online?

The value that many retailers provide to customers traditionally has come from the quality of their in-store service. Consider the Chinese cosmetics company Lin Qingxuan. It suffered a 90 percent collapse in store sales after the outbreak, when many locations were forced to close and others saw foot traffic plummet. In response, the company developed a strategy for digital engagement with customers that would replace the store experience: it turned the company's in-store beauty advisers into online influencers. The success of this move has prompted more investment in digital channels. Thanks to that and similar changes, Lin Qingxuan's increased online sales have more than made up for the fall in store sales during the crisis, notably in hard-hit Wuhan.

Which platforms should you work with?

The pandemic-induced shift to digital shopping has made customers and firms more dependent on big digital platforms, including Google, Amazon, and Apple in the West and Alibaba and Tencent in Asia, along with a newer group of aggressive rivals such as China's Meituan, Russia's Yandex, and Singapore's Grab. Increasingly, a firm's competitive space will be determined by the platform it works with. As retailers seek to carve out a distinctive position for themselves, they will have to learn to work with such platforms to innovate and shape their value propositions. For example, Lin Qingxuan's conversion of shop assistants into online influencers involved working in close partnership with Alibaba. The choice of platform to partner with should be driven by its ability to help you develop the strategic digital capabilities and resources you need to provide value online.

Can you expand your customer niche?

Digitization provides scope for niche businesses to expand their markets, perhaps across borders or into adjacencies not currently well served. Take the case of VIPKid, one of China's unicorns, which links teachers in English-speaking countries with Chinese children who want to learn English. With teaching switching from physical to online, the company has seen an opportunity to expand and deepen its links both with students in China and with teachers in the United States, Canada, and the U.K. Niche companies in other industries may find potential for online offerings in segments already being served by strong digital providers because of a selective wariness toward Big Tech that has become more apparent during the crisis. The distribution platform Bookshop.org, for example, links up independent bookstores that are worried about being exploited or ignored by Amazon. My Local Token also taps into a desire for alternatives to Big Tech, providing a cryptocurrency that enables local merchants to lower transaction fees, build customer loyalty, and reinvigorate small businesses. Ventures like these, whose value proposition is rooted in opposition to the network-maximizing ethos of Big Tech firms, could be described as Alt-Tech.

For the vast majority of companies, responding to demand shifts will involve at least some digital transformation—and probably a significant level of it. Microsoft CEO Satya Nadella observed at the end of April, "We have seen two years' worth of digital transformation in two months" among enterprise customers—and the result of those investments will persist long after the crisis. Employees at companies across the board have adjusted to working remotely and collaborating via video conferences. Many of those habits and patterns will stick.

Together, these factors explain why, in a survey of Fortune 500 CEOs, 63 percent said the Covid-19 crisis would accelerate their technological investment despite financial pressures. Only 6 percent said it would slow it down. But to make a difference, those IT investments should focus on specific business-model innovations to address new opportunities rather than increase the use of digital technologies in general.

Reallocate Your Capital

It may be psychologically hard to do during a crisis, when cash flows are stressed, but now is precisely the time to take a few well-considered risks. Research shows that the most successful companies not only invest more than their peers in new opportunities but also put their eggs in fewer baskets, devoting more than 90 percent of net spending to segments with higher growth and returns. These companies recognize that a crisis offers an opportunity to carve out a new competitive position.

Unfortunately, many companies are still defaulting to traditional habits of "peanut-buttering" new funding across the business and, when necessary, making horizontal cuts rather than targeted ones. According to BCG's survey of leading firms, as of May 2020 only 39 percent of companies had modified their investment and capital allocation plans to target new growth drivers, and of that minority, only half had made investments in new business models.

To avoid that trap, evaluate your capital investment projects along two dimensions: their estimated value tomorrow, after taking into account the impact of demand shifts, and the amount of money needed to keep them alive today in light of often-constrained operational cash flows. You can do this at the business unit level, but ideally you should dive deeper to examine specific operations or initiatives. Once you've completed this exercise, you'll most likely realize that you need to radically reallocate your capital investment.

In the current environment, larger corporations that are willing to entertain some risks are likely to benefit the most. Financial markets and institutions will be less ready or able to provide capital to smaller firms and start-ups right now. This means that large, established firms with relatively strong cash flows, and more access to capital as a result, will be well placed to take advantage of the opportunities afforded by shifts in demand.

But large companies need to be prepared to take on those risks. Rather than hoard cash and agonize about what might befall a particular sector or geographic region, CEOs should engage in more-aggressive dynamic capital investment. Heightened uncertainty means that organizations cannot accurately predict which businesses will be most successful tomorrow, so they need to take an experimental approach and take steps to diversify their portfolios to include a range of potential bets. The rapid pace of change means that they should frequently update their portfolios, reallocating funding as needed while making sure that they are balanced over time and fit the companies' long-term strategic priorities.

American Express has set the standard in this regard. During the 2008 global financial crisis, Amex was severely threatened by increasing defaults, decreasing consumer spending, and limited access to funding. The company launched a restructuring program to streamline the organization and reduce cash drain, and it entered into the deposit-gathering business in order to raise more capital. Those moves freed up or generated cash that Amex then directed toward longer-term investments in new partnerships and technology, which reimagined the company as not just a card provider but a platform-supported services company. As then-CEO Ken Chenault noted, "Even as we've cut operating expenses, we have continued to fund major growth initiatives." As a result, Amex's market capitalization grew more than 10-fold after the crisis.

Conclusion

In times of crisis, it's easy for organizations to default to old habits—but those are often the times in which new approaches are most valuable. As companies position themselves for the new normal, they cannot afford to be constrained by traditional information sources, business models, and capital allocation behaviors. Instead they must highlight anomalies and challenge mental models, revamp their business models, and invest their capital dynamically to not only survive the crisis but also thrive in the post-crisis world.

TAKEAWAYS

Crises produce not just temporary changes in customer behavior but also some lasting ones. Companies seeking to emerge from this crisis in a stronger position should reassess their growth opportunities in the new normal, reconfigure their business models to better realize those opportunities, and reallocate their capital accordingly.

- ✓ Unless we sensitize ourselves to new habits and their cascading indirect effects, we will fail to spot weak signals and miss opportunities to shape markets. Challenge traditional ideas, take multiple perspectives, and use data to actively seek out anomalies and surprises.

- ✓ Adjust your business model to reflect behavioral changes, considering what the new trends might mean for how you create and deliver value, whom you need to partner with, and who your customers should be.

- ✓ Put your money where your analysis takes you and be prepared to make aggressive, dynamic investments.

Adapted from "Adapt Your Business to the New Reality" in Harvard Business Review *September–October 2020 (product #R2005E).*

AVOID MAKING THIS STRATEGIC MISTAKE IN A RECESSION

by Michael Greiner and Scott Julian

W e are currently in the midst of the most severe economic crisis since the Great Depression. If this is purely a supply shock, then our economy should recover quickly once restrictions on economic activity are lifted. On the other hand, according to a report from the Becker Friedman Institute of the University of Chicago, 42 percent of the jobs lost so far in this crisis could be permanent losses. If that is the case, then this supply shock will turn into a demand crisis much like the Great Recession of 2008, and recovery will be much slower. With so much uncertainty, what should a strategist do?

We looked at data from the period right before the 2008 recession addressing how 5,278 publicly traded firms fared based on their generic strategy of being either pure differentiators or pure cost leaders, according to Michael Porter's theories. Differentiators compete based on a variety of factors, such as quality or service, rather than prioritizing low prices. Cost leaders, on the other hand, focus their strategy on reducing costs, thus enabling them to offer the product for the lowest possible price. Porter says either strategy will be successful as long as the strategic orientation is pure. But in our analysis, differentiators were significantly more likely to suffer reduced revenues than cost leaders in the Great Recession and were significantly more likely to go out of business.

In light of this, a thoughtful strategist might think it wise to change strategies by moving toward cost leadership. After all, moving from differentiation toward cost leadership makes a certain sense; everyone tightens their belts in a recession, particularly a severe one. Consumers reduce their spending and look for cheaper suppliers. Businesses seek to reduce their expenses to weather the storm. Especially in an environment as unpredictable as we had in 2008 (or as we have now), cutting costs becomes a central focus of most businesses' efforts. However, our data do not support changing strategies to become a cost leader during a recession. We found that when differentiators moved toward a cost leadership strategy such efforts did not help them. In fact, we found that changing strategy did not increase a firm's chances of surviving the recession, nor did it improve the firm's revenues or its finances.

This is the lesson of the Great Recession for strategists: cost leaders have a head start. As both kinds of firms seek to reduce costs to survive and reduce prices to attract more cost-conscious customers, cost leaders have the advantage because they are structured for such an approach. This is exactly the problem to which Porter pointed. In a competition to become more of a cost leader, the cost leader always wins. So, what should a differentiator do? Our research does point to some concrete lessons for strategists at differentiator firms during recessions.

First, do not try to change strategies. A differentiator will never out-cost leader a cost leader. As a result, differentiators are better off focusing and trying to build on their strengths. Next, reduce costs quickly, to a point. When faced with uncertain demand, firms need to lower costs as quickly as possible in an effort to marshal resources for a long fight back. Waiting to reduce costs in the hope that the recovery comes quickly will put a firm in a difficult position if that gamble turns out to be wrong. At the same time, the firm must be careful that these cuts do not jeopardize its ability to deliver a differentiated product or service. Finally, know that there is no easy solution. Simply reducing prices will not solve the problem. Unless you are the industry's low-cost leader, there will always be someone who can provide your goods or services at a lower price. Therefore, you need to mine the entrepreneurial fire that helped build your firm in the first place. Focus on your strengths. The advantages that made your product or service worth more than what the cost leaders offer still apply. You just need to make that case to your customers.

The good news is that most firms did survive the 2008 Great Recession. You might lead one of those firms. If that is the case, you know exactly what kind of hard work is required to survive a crisis of this magnitude. Imagining the grass to be greener for those following a strategy very different from yours, however, is not a viable solution.

TAKEAWAYS

Analysis of the Great Recession shows that companies with a strategic orientation of *pure differentiator* were significantly more likely than *pure cost leaders* to suffer reduced revenues or go out of business. Even so, firms that changed strategy from differentiator to cost leader in the recession did not increase their chances of survival, nor did it improve their revenues or its finances.

- ✓ Don't try to out-cost leader a cost leader; differentiators will have better success by focusing and trying to build on their strengths.

- ✓ Lower expenses as quickly as possible to marshal resources for a long fight back. Waiting to reduce costs in the hope that the recovery comes quickly will put your firm in a difficult position if that gamble turns out to be wrong.

- ✓ Mine the entrepreneurial fire that helped build your firm in the first place. Focus on your strengths. The advantages that made your product or service worth more than what the cost leaders offer still apply.

Adapted from "Avoid Making This Strategic Mistake in a Recession" on hbr.org, July 23, 2020 (product #H05PV9).

Section 2

MANAGING YOUR BUSINESS THROUGH THE RECESSION

3

WHAT REALLY PREVENTS COMPANIES FROM THRIVING IN A RECESSION

by Ranjay Gulati and Mark Wiedman

Business leaders know they should "never let a good crisis go to waste," but very few of them actually live this maxim. In a study of companies' performance during and after the past several recessions, one of us found that 17 percent didn't survive (because they filed for bankruptcy, were acquired, or went private), and of those that did, the vast majority—80 percent—were still struggling three years later to match their pre-recession growth.[1] Only 9 percent of surviving companies "roared out of the recession," posting results that exceeded both their peers' and their pre-recession performance. These firms managed a delicate dance, playing both offense (investing in growth opportunities including new businesses) and defense (cutting costs and finding operational efficiencies) in response to external shifts. Even while reducing overall spending, they were able to carve out resources for new endeavors.

Aware of the need to respond more adroitly to sudden shocks, leaders have since pushed to make their companies flatter, more "agile," and more "disruption proof." Yet even firms that have adopted these approaches struggle to respond quickly and proactively enough when crises arise. In our research and personal experience, we've found that the problem is ultimately a systemic one. Your strategic posture depends on how you deploy your resources, so to truly leverage a crisis to your advantage, you must change basic processes of resource allocation in your organization.

Even in the best of times, many companies fail to fund and staff new opportunities, and not for lack of good ideas. Some leaders at public companies blame investor pressures—the "capitalizing versus expensing" dilemma. In their view, markets favor companies that take a hit on their balance sheet for acquisitions (capitalizing) over companies that present poor income statements thanks to increased spending on internal innovation projects (expensing). In practice, it's often easier to make a $1 billion acquisition than to find $10 million to internally respond to or prepare for market shifts.

This seemingly reasonable explanation fails under scrutiny. Leaders could seize new opportunities not by increasing expenses overall but by shifting existing funds, leaving their income statements untouched. And yet, most of the time, they refuse to make even mild changes in existing budgets. This, many leaders like to argue, has to do with concrete budget calculations and processes. These decisions hinge, after all, on quantified analysis of projected internal rates of return. New opportunities, exciting as they might be, simply fail to meet existing thresholds for risk. When leaders run the numbers, adapting to change seems like a bad bet.

But this explanation also falls flat, for it assumes that organizations are perfectly rational places where Excel spreadsheets and ROIs rule the day. Quantification of risk or return isn't as easy or reliable as it might seem nor does it truly drive decision making. Rather, leaders often make choices based on impressions and enthusiasms—gut feeling, intuition. Much of the time, projected numbers are simply used to justify and socialize their preferences.

To understand why large organizations don't always invest in new opportunities and hence why they struggle to play both offense and defense when crises arise, we must analyze the emotions that bear on resource allocation decisions. For reallocation to happen, *deallocation* must also occur. As decades of research have shown, leaders fear threats to their status and power and so become attached to existing businesses and budgets, regarding them as entitlements and as a baseline for determining what's "fair."

Leaders fear losing not only money but also people and focus. Individual business owners within an enterprise want to protect the top talent they have wherever they are rather than shift them to different areas or bring in new people. Or maybe they've built a strategy around certain things and worry that trying anything else will divert too much time and energy from the core.

The emotional dynamics leading to inertia in budgeting become amplified in some contexts more than others. Companies that focus on delivering "premium" offerings to customers, for instance, may have a harder time diverting scarce resources away from existing operations. Their attention remains fixed on adding value, even in areas that might not matter to customers. Subtraction just isn't in their DNA.

So, what might break the lethargy in firms? An external trauma or force, such as a global pandemic or other crisis event, certainly helps. But here are two key measures leaders might adopt to further enhance their agility and flexibility in times of crisis so that they can play both offense and defense effectively.

First, leaders can *set the strategic frame* for resource reallocation decisions. By focusing people on a positive vision of the future rather than holding onto what they have done in the past, they can foster more alignment for future reallocation of resources. Entrenched turf battles deescalate, moderating the fears deallocation can trigger. Assurances of safety and security can further tamp down fears.

Leaders can also break the mentality of entitlement by *reforming the budgeting process.* With the strategic frame firmly in place, they should lay out new "rules of the game" for resource decisions, delineating which types of projects the organization will and will not fund and what metrics will be used to evaluate both existing and potential projects. At the extreme, they might force change by breaking the connection between budgets from year to year, establishing that only perhaps 70 percent to 80 percent of the previous annual budget will carry over. Publicly committing to ranges allays fears by capping how much existing units and team heads stand to lose.

Reallocation isn't the only answer for companies, either. When faced with a declining business, leaders might decide to simply run it down, expanding their margins and returning cash to shareholders. Although leaders usually shrink from this option, it too stands as a legitimate choice in certain situations. What isn't legitimate is the default at most organizations today: stubbornly investing in the same old ways even as markets change.

H. G. Wells famously wrote: "Adapt or perish, now as ever, is nature's inexorable imperative." Covid-19 will not be the last crisis to confront global business with this choice—maybe not even the last this year. To protect your company, you must go beyond relatively superficial reforms such as implementation of agile structures and instead address the internal dynamics that affect how the organization deploys resources. Leaders must prod themselves free from the powerful emotional forces that prevent them from a readiness to respond to and innovate in crisis. If you want a vaccine that will inoculate you against the ever-shifting threats posed by volatility, this is the best you've got.

TAKEAWAYS

Even in the best of times, many companies fail to fund and staff new opportunities and make changes in existing budgets. An external trauma or force, such as a global pandemic or other crisis event, can break this lethargy and help companies embrace agility.

✓ Two key measures can enhance companies' flexibility further:

- *Setting the strategic frame* for resource reallocation decisions by focusing people on a positive vision of the future.

- *Reforming the budgeting process* by establishing new metrics that will be used to evaluate both existing and potential projects.

✓ Reallocation isn't the only answer. When faced with a declining business, leaders might decide to simply run it down, expanding their margins and returning cash to shareholders.

NOTE

1. Ranjay Gulati, Nitin Nohria, and Franz Wohlgezogen, "Roaring Out of Recession," *Harvard Business Review*, March 2010, https:// hbr.org/2010/03/roaring-out-of-recession.

Adapted from "What Really Prevents Companies from Thriving in a Recession" on hbr.org, September 2, 2020 (product #H05UA6).

4

DO YOU HAVE THE RIGHT SALES CHANNELS FOR A DOWNTURN?

by Andris A. Zoltners, Prabhakant Sinha, Sally E. Lorimer, and John DeSarbo

Major economic downturns hit most companies. And manufacturers who sell to their customers through channel partners, such as retailers or value-added resellers, face additional challenges. Undercapitalized partners may be unable to get products to customers—or worse, could go bust. With the current pandemic, the situation appears dire, with even more bankruptcies predicted than occurred during the global financial crisis of 2008–2009.

For manufacturers, success when emerging from a major downturn requires rethinking channel strategy. Manufacturers who simply plot a "return to the way it was" may not fare well.

Across industries, hard-hit channel partners have scrambled to respond to the pandemic. They've cut costs through furloughs, layoffs, reduced inventory levels, and delayed capital investments. Government programs (such as the CARES Act in the United States) have provided temporary relief for many. And better-capitalized manufacturers have stepped in to help struggling channel partners. More than half of technology manufacturers extended payment terms. Cisco offered partners $2.5 billion in additional financing. Dell and others followed suit. But even with manufacturers stepping up to help, many channel partners will not survive.

Manufacturers should ask three questions as they rethink channel strategies and programs to drive both short-term and long-term success through the recovery.

#1: Is it time to change channel mix and responsibilities?

Following a downturn, it's tempting for manufacturers to attempt to revert to their past channel strategies. Yet evolving customer needs make this an opportune time to rethink channel mix and responsibilities. Some situations call for more direct selling to customers while others call for an increased role for channel partners.

More direct selling. To address changes in consumer behavior during the pandemic, PepsiCo launched a direct-to-consumer channel allowing customers to buy their favorite brands online. Channel preferences are also changing in B2B sectors as customers seek to reduce pandemic-induced supply chain disruptions by cutting out the middleman. Manufacturers can respond by expanding direct selling to their larger indirect customers. Manufacturers can also create hybrid models in which they take back some channel responsibilities such as product promotion or logistics.

More selling through channel partners. While some manufacturers expand their direct sales footprint, others will find it's time to do the opposite. L. L. Bean recently announced it will begin selling indirectly for the first time—partnerships with Nordstrom, Scheels, and Staples will enable it to expand its market coverage and reach underserved customer segments. Manufacturers serving businesses also have an opportunity to leverage new indirect channels. As business customers, like consumers, boost online purchasing, digital marketplaces such as Zoro.com and Amazon Business become more attractive.

Selecting the optimal channel strategy requires understanding what customers value, assessing manufacturer and partner capabilities, and analyzing channel economics.

#2: Are you investing in the right channel partners?

Emerging from the downturn, manufacturers will be tempted to prioritize partners who were successful in the past. Their perspective reflects singer Shania Twain's refrain, "You got to dance with the one that brought you." However, yesterday's winners could be tomorrow's stragglers. To remain viable, some previously successful partners delayed investments in hiring, training, and IT and do not have access to capital to expand operations quickly. There is a risk that these under-resourced partners will become overly reliant on manufacturer support, thereby driving up manufacturer channel costs.

To win over the long term, manufacturers must invest in partners who provide what customers value. Partners, no doubt, are also looking for manufacturers with winning offerings, incentives, and support programs. Some situations call for manufacturers to double down on the largest partners while others necessitate shifting investment to smaller up-and-coming partners.

Investing in the largest, strongest partners. Relying on a fragmented network of small, undercapitalized partners could slow the rebound. Now could be the time to focus on partners best positioned for future success. Nearly 20 years ago, farm equipment manufacturer John Deere launched its "Dealer of Tomorrow" program to reward dealers who invested in the capabilities that larger farms demanded while de-emphasizing dealers who did not fit this desired profile. The program significantly improved customer service and dramatically reduced the number of dealers.

Helping smaller up-and-coming partners. Some manufacturers will find that, coming out of a downturn, better-capitalized partners gain too much power. Larger partners may drive smaller partners out of business, creating coverage gaps and unstable customer relationships. Large partners also gain leverage in price negotiations with manufacturers, leading to margin compression. In 2001, building materials manufacturer Cemex mitigated such risks by launching Construrama to support small, independent hardware retailers in Mexico and Central America. Cemex helped these retailers compete against increasingly powerful big box stores by providing training, sales and marketing support, and IT systems. In exchange, Construrama retailers agreed to meet service standards and promote Cemex products. Today, Cemex has a massive building materials distribution network, with 2,300+ Construrama stores.

#3: Should you change channel compensation and incentives?

As demand returns, manufacturers will be tempted to ramp up sales by offering partners lower prices if they commit to increased order volumes. This strategy can be risky, however. Volume-based discounts can inadvertently motivate partners to overbuy, creating working capital challenges. Such partners will then request payment-term extensions, thus increasing channel costs.

Volume-based incentives also give larger partners an unfair advantage, thereby fostering price erosion and accelerating undesired channel consolidation.

Now is the time to consider overdue changes to channel partner compensation programs by reexamining partner pay levels and the behaviors and outcomes tied to compensation.

Changing pay levels to reflect changing roles. Some manufacturers have not significantly changed channel pricing and incentives for years, despite changing partner responsibilities. Increases or reductions in channel responsibilities must be reflected in the compensation structure. In the consumer products industry, with sales through digital retailers skyrocketing, more manufacturers are holding inventory and shipping products directly to customers and reducing channel compensation accordingly. On the other hand, in the enterprise software industry, manufacturers offer channel partners additional deal registration incentives for independently acquiring new customers without manufacturer support.

Investing to drive the right behaviors. Manufacturer incentives, such as functional discounts and co-funding, can motivate specific partner behaviors. For example, in some industries, partners have resisted manufacturer requests for point-of-sale data. By rewarding partners for data sharing, manufacturers improve visibility into customer needs. Other manufacturers use incentives to motivate investment in new capabilities. Technology leaders such as Microsoft, Cisco, and HP have reengineered partner programs to reward reseller expertise and coverage in high-potential sectors (for example, healthcare) and in-demand technologies (for example, advanced analytics, cybersecurity).

Stanford economist Paul Romer once said, "a crisis is a terrible thing to waste." Serious economic downturns provide opportunity for manufacturers to rethink channel strategies for a changing world.

TAKEAWAYS

Manufacturers that sell their products through channels such as retailers or value-added resellers must rethink their strategies as the recession continues. They should consider three main questions as they reevaluate channel strategies.

✓ **Is it time to change channel mix and responsibilities?** This may result in more direct selling or more selling through channel partners.

✓ **Are you investing in the right channel partners?** Some situations call for manufacturers to double down on their largest partners while others necessitate shifting investment to smaller up-and-coming partners.

✓ **Should you change channel compensation and incentives?** Now is the time to consider overdue changes to channel partner compensation programs. Change pay levels to reflect changing roles and invest funds to drive the right behaviors.

Adapted from "Do You Have the Right Sales Channels for a Downturn?" on hbr.org, September 4, 2020 (product #H05U51).

5

JOINT VENTURES AND PARTNERSHIPS IN A DOWNTURN

by James Bamford, Gerard Baynham, and David Ernst

ompanies will need every tool they've got to survive the downturn and rev up their businesses as
the economy rights itself. They'll have to rewire operations, reallocate resources, and in some cases reinvent
business models.

At many firms, joint ventures and partnerships will play
an outsize role in those efforts, both as a vehicle for sharing costs and reducing capital needs during the crisis and

as a way to position themselves for growth once it ends. After all, in industries experiencing great pressure—like automotive, retail, and upstream oil and gas—joint ventures (JVs) are quite common. GM and Volkswagen, for example, each have several dozen, and JVs account for almost 80 percent of the upstream production of the largest international oil and gas companies. At these and other energy businesses, joint ventures are also key to managing the transition from fossil fuels to renewables. More than 50 percent of the largest assets in offshore wind and solar are structured as joint ventures—and such investments are a critical way for companies like Royal Dutch Shell, BP, Total, and Equinor to share risks, build capabilities, and meet ambitious targets to reduce greenhouse gas emissions.

In healthcare and life sciences, joint ventures and partnerships are crucial to innovation: more than two-thirds of new health insurance products in the United States are built on co-branded or JV offerings, while life sciences companies depend on such ventures to accelerate time to market and broaden distribution of lifesaving products. In March 2020, for instance, Pfizer and BioNTech announced they were teaming up to bring out a Covid-19 vaccine. Other partnerships aimed at developing Covid-19 vaccines have been announced by Sanofi and GSK and by Hoth Therapeutics, Voltron Therapeutics, and Mass General Hospital.

JVs now drive a material share of companies' profits as well. In 2019 Airbus, Celanese, Engie, Vodafone, and Volkswagen relied on noncontrolled JVs for more than 20 percent of their earnings while at Coca-Cola, GM, and many others that figure was above 10 percent.

Moving forward, we expect the impact of JVs and partnerships to remain significant and, in some sectors and geographies, to increase. We recently analyzed trends related to joint ventures across the past 35 years. Our analysis showed that in most industries, terminations of them didn't always increase during downturns—and often fell. Use of JVs also tended to rise on the eve of a recovery. This may be partly due to the time it takes to negotiate a restructuring or an exit as well as corporate management's tendency to look first to wholly owned operations when cutting costs. In addition, JVs' returns on assets have been climbing recently—and are higher than those of wholly owned companies in the same industries. That means the number of terminations during this economic dip is likely to be even lower. Meanwhile, our analysis also showed that new joint venture and partnership transactions tend to increase during a downturn and to accelerate during a recovery because they allow companies to get off to a much quicker start than organic growth does and are less risky than M&A.

In this chapter we'll look at how during this period of retrenchment firms might stabilize their existing

FIGURE 5-1

Terminations don't always increase during recessions and decline afterward.

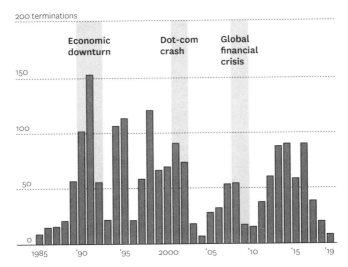

Source: SDC Platinum, public announcements; analysis by Water Street Partners.
Note: Chart plots 1,873 JV terminations; non-JV partnerships excluded.

joint ventures by raising cash, cutting operating costs, reducing capital spending, managing risk, and restructuring. These are commonsense moves for the most part, but they require sustained focus; JVs are hard to restructure even in the best of times, owing to differing owner-company agendas, politicized processes, and general inertia. However, a crisis can serve as a catalyst

FIGURE 5-2

Joint ventures' ROA is higher than the ROA of similar investments.

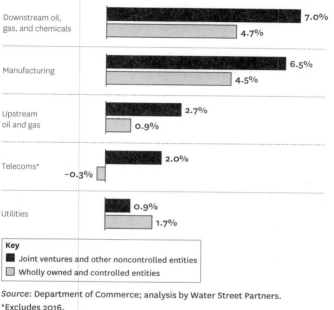

Downstream oil, gas, and chemicals — 7.0% / 4.7%

Manufacturing — 6.5% / 4.5%

Upstream oil and gas — 2.7% / 0.9%

Telecoms* — 2.0% / −0.3%

Utilities — 0.9% / 1.7%

Key
- Joint ventures and other noncontrolled entities
- Wholly owned and controlled entities

Source: Department of Commerce; analysis by Water Street Partners.
*Excludes 2016.

Note: Based on an analysis of 20,000-plus investments, 2014 to 2017. Investments include JVs, mergers and acquisitions, and organic growth.

for change. In addition, we'll look at how companies might enter into new "counter-downturn" JVs and partnerships, both to manage the challenging economic environment and to tap into growth opportunities in capital-light ways.

Shoring Up Existing JVs

Joint ventures are facing many of the same financial challenges—severe revenue shortfalls from fractured supply chains, curtailed operations, evaporating market demand, and frozen credit markets—as their owners and wholly owned peers. These new economic realities require both short- and long-term responses.

Efforts to reduce working capital, cut costs, tap additional credit lines, and take advantage of government subsidies and relief programs are already well under way in most joint ventures. To help pull off these near-term interventions, their boards will need to get far more involved than usual. Under normal conditions, joint ventures' board directors spend an average of 5 percent to 10 percent of their time on governance. But during economic storms, an effective board can be the factor that determines whether a JV thrives, stagnates, or dies an untimely death. Working with managers, directors are convening special board and committee meetings and fast-tracking decisions.

JV partners, boards, and management teams will also need to evaluate opportunities to more fundamentally reset their businesses. Because of their shared ownership, joint ventures can use restructuring tools that aren't available to wholly owned businesses. These approaches may benefit a venture, its parents, or both. They come in various forms.

Raising capital in unconventional ways.

Some joint ventures will have opportunities to secure low-interest or interest-free loans or capital from their cash-rich owners—such as state-owned companies, sovereign wealth funds, private equity (PE) firms, and multinationals with strong balance sheets. In exchange, those owners might get additional interest in the venture, preferred returns, or increased control. In 2015, when Russian automobile sales collapsed amid wider economic problems, Ford Sollers, a 50–50 joint venture between Ford and Sollers PJSC, received additional funding from Ford, which in return got preferred shares that gave it majority voting rights.

To free up cash, improve future liquidity, or open up new markets, joint ventures may also want to bring in new owners, such as PE firms, pension funds, other financial institutions or strategic industry partners. Earnouts for the current owners could be pegged to the future performance of the business to make adding more owners attractive. Many investors, like PE firms, can bring in capabilities that give ventures a boost, including a better understanding of value creation; a sharp focus on cost reduction and talent management; governance discipline; M&A experience; and a portfolio that can double as an ecosystem of customers, suppliers, or partners.

Structuring creative commercial arrangements with suppliers, customers, lenders, and other business partners is another option for JV owners. In the past we've seen an ownership interest or option sold to a major supplier or customer in exchange for better commercial terms, including cash advances. If one of the owners is a major supplier to the JV, the parties might renegotiate their agreement (to, say, narrow the band of prices). Similarly, a joint venture might negotiate with a lender to convert debt to equity, making the creditor a direct owner.

Reducing costs through synergies and new operating models.

While JVs can cut costs on their own, much greater savings may come from consolidating or otherwise optimizing activities and assets with their owners. Ventures and owners might make joint purchases, integrate their supply chains, or combine some infrastructure, logistics, warehouses, or other operating assets. In 2003, Vodafone entered an agreement with SFR, its French mobile-telecommunications JV with Vivendi, to collaborate to improve economies of scale in operational areas like the development and rollout of new offerings and procurement, especially of technology.

Joint ventures might also save money by insourcing certain functions (such as legal, HR, IT, or finance) currently being provided by an owner. Our analysis has shown that although owner companies rarely profit from providing administrative services to joint ventures, their cost structures are often 10 percent to 30 percent higher than those of the JVs or of third-party providers they might contract with. Conversely, a joint venture that lacks scale might benefit from outsourcing certain functions to an owner or a third party.

In some cases cost cutting may lead to more-fundamental changes to the operating model. Those that reduce operating expenses or increase strategic and financial flexibility are especially popular during downturns. A lower-cost partner in a joint venture or a third party might become the controlling partner or operator, which can open up synergies with that organization. In our view many joint ventures should aggressively pursue this option, which allows greater nimbleness and offers more potential for performance improvement than do JV models in which control is shared by the partners and the joint venture's management doesn't have much authority.

In response to the Asian financial crisis in the late 1990s, BASF and Mitsubishi creatively restructured their equally owned and controlled joint venture in Japan, Mitsubishi Chemical BASF. It was split into two joint ventures, one focused on dispersants and the other on foam products—the business's two core segments. Each was placed under the operational leadership of the parent best positioned to strengthen it—with BASF responsible for the dispersants venture and Mitsubishi responsible for the foam products one.

Regearing financial ratios.

Joint venture boards might also consider authorizing or compelling management to increase external borrowing, especially if the entity is underleveraged, as JVs tend to be. Conversely, if a venture has excess cash, the board might seek to repatriate it to fund other pressing corporate needs. During the 2008 financial crisis, the board of a large liquefied-natural-gas JV found that it had almost $500 million in cash on hand—enough to cover six months of operating costs. The board immediately approved a $300 million dividend, giving the owners cash to weather the storm elsewhere in their businesses.

Assisting owners through buyouts and other means.

Downturns tend to expose strategy and performance differences among partners. While the data doesn't suggest they cause buyouts to spike, inevitably there will be some buyouts and sellouts, and some JVs will be terminated or liquidated.

In the current environment, routine decisions about budgets and capital expenditures may become deadlocked, triggering buy-sell options in about a third of joint venture contracts. In other cases the potential synergies will be greater if a single partner has full ownership, and the one for whom the JV is more core—or already more integrated—will buy out the other partners. Or one owner might acquire and integrate parts of the joint venture or sell out to a third party. After the 2008–2009 financial crisis forced the Canadian company Nortel to file for bankruptcy protection, for example, it sold its controlling stake in a high-performing Korean joint venture with LG to Ericsson. Alternatively, all the owners might sell the venture to a consortium of financial investors.

Creating New Joint Ventures and Partnerships

New JVs and partnerships can also help companies navigate the economic crisis. They can be used to raise cash, secure cost synergies, or pursue lower-risk and more-capital-efficient growth. When funding is tight, such benefits make joint ventures and partnerships a popular alternative to mergers and acquisitions or organic investments. Our analysis shows that JVs and partnerships tend to increase in the late stages of a downturn, signaling a recovery and outpacing M&A. Right after the 1990–1992 and 2001–2002 downturns, for instance, the number of new joint ventures and partnership transactions was 20 percent above normal levels.

Partial divestments.

For companies that need more liquidity, a joint venture can be a good alternative to a full divestiture. One approach is to use it as the first step in a planned exit: A seller puts a noncore business into a joint venture with a potential buyer and negotiates to sell the full business over time, typically within three to five years. This kind of deal is especially worthwhile for sellers when prospective buyers don't recognize the full potential of the business or its assets or may not be able to buy or operate the business on day one. IBM used this staged-exit structure when it sold its personal computer business to Lenovo, and so did Lanxess when it folded its specialty plastics business into a joint venture with Ineos, in 2007. In that case, Lanxess received one payment when the joint venture was set up and a second after two years, when it fully exited the JV. The second payment was based on the performance of the business—a useful method when it's difficult to arrive at a valuation.

Another approach is to sell a partial interest in a business unit to a third party, effectively converting the business into a joint venture. Dow Chemical famously pursued such a game-changing structure in 2008, when it tried to sell key elements of its commodity-chemical business to Kuwait's state-owned Petrochemicals Industry Company to raise cash and reduce exposure to the cyclical commodity-chemical business. But it was left at the altar when the Kuwaiti parliament rejected the deal at the last minute. During the Asian financial crisis, Doosan agreed to sell a 50 percent interest in its Oriental Brewery unit to the global player Interbrew to raise cash. The deal gave Oriental Brewery access to new technologies, marketing networks, and cost management capabilities that lifted its performance. In a similar move, from 2008 to 2010, Chesapeake Energy raised more than $8 billion by selling a partial interest in its U.S. shale gas assets to BP, Equinor, Total, and others.

A creative third alternative is an asset sale with a lease-back. Through such deals, companies typically divest certain (noncore) assets but tie them to a joint venture. For instance, as part of an aggressive corporate restructuring program it ran from 2005 to 2007, Sony sold its chip-manufacturing facilities to Toshiba for more than $800 million; those assets were then leased back to a new joint venture between the companies, which produced chips for the PlayStation and other Sony consumer electronics.

Business consolidations.

Synergies from this kind of joint venture can be substantial. There is a range of options here. At the narrower end of the spectrum, companies (especially those in the natural resources sector) consolidate a set of adjacent assets into a single joint venture to align all the parties' incentives better and save money on infrastructure. Extending that logic more broadly to an entire region, country, or business unit, companies can consolidate similar operations with those of an industry peer or competitor to capture additional scale or cost synergies. In 2009 Morgan

Stanley and Citibank consolidated their retail brokerage and wealth management businesses into a 51–49 joint venture in which Citibank also received an up-front cash payment of $2.7 billion. In a similar vein, in 2013 Bertelsmann and Pearson combined their trade-book publishing businesses, which were facing headwinds, into a 53–47 joint venture, Penguin Random House.

Companies might also team up with industry peers to consolidate back-office, sales, or purchasing functions into joint ventures and realize greater economies of scale. The big three U.S. automakers have done this in forming global purchasing joint ventures. Oil and gas companies have also pursued purchasing cooperatives, logistics pooling, shared maintenance and inventory management ventures, and other collaborative structures. So have telecom companies. For instance, Deutsche Telekom and France Télécom-Orange formed BuyIn, a purchasing joint venture in which the companies pooled procurement activities in an effort to save more than a billion dollars annually.

Partnerships for capital-light growth.

Companies looking for growth but seeking lower investment risk can consider a range of transaction structures. Some firms may enter global strategic partnerships with cash-rich players—including state-owned companies, sovereign wealth funds, or PE firms—to identify and develop a portfolio of opportunities within a sector or a market. The global oil corporation BP, the European chemicals maker Borealis, the Brazilian state-owned oil company Petrobras, and the French automaker Renault are among the dozens of companies that have pursued such arrangements over the years.

Alternatively, companies might acquire a partial stake in troubled business units of their peers operating in attractive markets. In 2003 the French oil giant Total took a 50 percent position in Samsung Chemicals through its chemicals unit Atofina, creating Samsung Atofina, to which it transferred technology, operating capabilities, and marketing expertise that jump-started the business's growth. In some cases firms might jointly acquire third parties, as competitors Votorantim and Suzano did when they bought majority voting control in the Brazilian pulp and paper maker company Ripasa during a market downturn. That transaction was structured to maintain the market independence of the two owners, converting Ripasa into a jointly controlled production unit. The agreement also provided the purchasers with the option to acquire additional preferred and common stock of Ripasa within six years.

A similar strategy is to invest in or partner with innovative suppliers and technology companies. Toyota's investments and deep partnerships with core parts suppliers in the 1990s were credited with compressing the time necessary to go from concept to production, reducing manufacturing costs, and lowering defects. Similarly, in the 1990s, Samsung Electronics developed a program that nurtured suppliers with financial support and help building their technical capabilities, which led to technology improvements, savings on materials, and shorter order lead times.

Today power, chemical, mining, and petroleum companies could set up similar deals, making minority investments in clean-tech, renewable energy, recycling, or autonomous vehicle firms and agreeing to pilot those firms' technologies in their operations. Such arrangements would allow large incumbents with lower price-to-earnings ratios to participate in firms with much higher growth prospects and valuations and to speed up their transition to a carbonless future.

Yet another approach is to team up with industry peers and adjacent players to create and commercialize new products. Within the chemical sector, companies have been forming consortia and small partnerships to establish standards for, develop, and sell new sustainable technologies. Similar patterns will play out in other sectors; partnerships are especially valuable in disruptive markets and on technology frontiers. Many of these will start as simple nonequity collaborations with an option to convert to a full-scale joint venture once certain technology or financial milestones are passed, as a way to hedge bets and reduce up-front investments.

Conclusion

As an epigram often attributed to Vladimir Lenin goes, "There are decades where nothing happens, and there are weeks where decades happen." In 2020 we have lived through a ridiculous number of those weeks. Yet periods of disruption can be rich in opportunity. A strategic examination of your current joint ventures and partnerships and the thoughtful creation of new ones can strengthen your position as you come out of the crisis and help you tap opportunities for growth during the coming rebound.

To make it through the downturn and return to growth, companies will need to rewire operations, reallocate resources, and in some cases reinvent business models. Joint ventures and partnerships can help many firms with those efforts.

✓ Companies can shore up their existing JVs through capital-raising, cost-reduction, and synergy-tapping techniques that often aren't available to wholly owned entities.

✓ Parent companies can strengthen their own financial positions by using JVs and partnerships to make partial divestments, consolidate businesses, and collaborate on capital-light, low-risk growth initiatives.

✓ JVs are already ubiquitous in sectors under pressure, such as energy, and in innovative industries, such as life sciences.

✓ At numerous firms, JVs drive a large share of earnings. Given that their returns have been climbing, their impact is quite likely to remain strong or even increase in the foreseeable future.

Adapted from "Joint Ventures and Partnerships in a Downturn," Harvard Business Review, *September–October 2020 (product #R2005K).*

DON'T CUT YOUR MARKETING BUDGET IN A RECESSION

by Nirmalya Kumar and Koen Pauwels

Most companies reduce spending in recessions, especially on marketing items that may be easier to cut (certainly relative to payroll). Right now, advertising agencies are struggling to stay afloat, and Google and Facebook are reporting substantially lower ad revenues as marketing spending dives with the business cycle (cyclical marketing). But that is today's equivalent of bleeding—an old-fashioned but once widespread treatment that actually reduces the patient's ability to fight disease.

Companies that have bounced back most strongly from previous recessions usually did not cut their marketing spend and, in many cases, actually increased it.[1] But they did change what they were spending their marketing budget on and when to reflect the new context in which they operated. Let's begin by taking a look at the various categories of marketing costs.

R&D and New Product Launches

New product launches are risky even in boom times, and there is always considerable debate within any firm about which of the many new products under development should actually go to market. In this context, axing new product development projects in a recession looks like a no-brainer.

But research in contexts as different as U.K. fast-moving consumer goods and U.S. automobile markets shows that products launched during a recession have both higher long-term survival chances and higher sales revenues.[2] That's partly because there are fewer new products to compete with, but it also comes from the fact that companies maintaining R&D have focused the investment on their best prospects—which may explain why products introduced during recessions have been shown to be of higher quality.

Timing, of course, is important: Our research shows that the best period to launch a new product is just after a recession's midpoint. This is when consumers start to think about nonnecessities, even expensive products they don't want to buy yet (such as cars). A new and innovative product engenders hope that the economy is on the mend and that the consumer may soon be able to afford it.

Even if they don't have new products ready to bring to market at the right time, smart firms continue to invest in R&D during recessions, which has been shown to have a stronger impact over long-term performance than other categories of marketing spending, such as advertising and price promotion.[3] This is because maintaining R&D means that companies emerge from the recession with a relatively stronger pipeline, particularly in cyclical industries such as automobiles, cement, and steel.

Prices and Promotions

Faced with declining sales volume, managers are tempted to increase prices in the hope of maintaining revenues and margins. It's not hard to see why this is a bad idea: as recessions make consumers more price sensitive, any increase in price will further reduce the likelihood of making a sale, which is why firms that have raised prices soon turn to price promotions to reverse the effect. But the research shows that this seesawing on price backfires: firms that engage in it lose more market share than those that don't.[4]

Communication

During recessions, when most firms are cutting back on their brand advertising, a firm's share of voice increases if it can maintain or increase its advertising budget. Take the case of Reckitt Benckiser: In the recession following the 2008 financial crash, the company launched a marketing campaign aimed at persuading its consumers to continue purchasing its more expensive and better-performing brands, despite the harsh economic climate. Increasing its advertising outlays by 25 percent in the face of reduced marketing by competitors, Reckitt Benckiser actually grew revenues by 8 percent and profits by 14 percent, when most of its rivals were reporting profit declines of 10 percent or more.[5] They viewed advertising as an investment rather than an expense.

The content of advertising during recessions must reflect the challenges that consumers are encountering. Consumers in a downturn want to see brands show solidarity. Successful brand advertising during a recession not only injects humor and emotion but also answers for consumers the question: How can we help?

Take the case of Coca-Cola. In 2020, the company used its advertising budget to showcase the work of frontline workers, creating mini stories about unsung heroes. The Coca-Cola brand features subtly in the background of these messages, reminding consumers that Coca-Cola always has been and always will be there for you, in good times and bad.

A similar tactic allowed Singapore Airlines to demonstrate how its grounded crew was redeployed to helping the community deal with the outbreak. Cabin crew used their skills as care ambassadors. Some helped nurses by taking patients' vital signs, noting meal orders, and serving them. Others worked at transport hubs assisting with crowd control and ensuring compliance with safe distancing guidelines.

Tailoring the Response to the Context

We all know that a company's existing branding and size are major factors in how well placed it is to weather and even benefit from a recession. Strong brands are often better able to maintain prices in a recession. At the same time, large companies and smart negotiators can often get price concessions from suppliers in a recession. But how a company's positioning and capability play out—and what needs to change—will depend on the dynamics of the industry and country in question, which means that companies operating in multiple markets need to choose different strategies for different parts of the business.

Take the case of one large Russian conglomerate that we advised during and after the 2008 global financial crisis. It operates in six countries and six industries, ranging from mainstream apparel to specialized banking. For its mainstream apparel brand in Russia, the company maintained its advertising budget while other (mostly foreign) brands simply cut the quantity of messaging and did little to change the content of what they did release. This worked out well for the company because its existing positioning as a local value-for-money brand appealed to consumers at a time when spending on foreign luxuries felt and looked bad. As the recession receded, many new customers, who had switched from more expensive foreign clothing, stayed with the local brand.

The conglomerate applied a very different approach to its banking operation in Romania. Unlike most of its competitors, our client expected a deep recession and a slow recovery. In this scenario the prospects for getting in new business were poor, and so the company slashed its previously large retail advertising budget and closed a large number of retail branches. This freed up resources so that it could better support existing customers. All customer acquisition efforts, meanwhile, were focused on high net-worth individuals. Its focus on helping existing customers and its careful targeting of new customers helped the bank to grow in the post-recession recovery period.

Marketing in a recession will never be easy, largely because it often involves going against instincts and standard operating norms. Customers' behavior undergoes profound changes—reflecting changes in their circumstances and needs, which may even be traumatic. In this environment you must accompany your customers on their new, different journey, shifting your message and even reengineering your value proposition. This is a time not to stop spending money but a time to change how you spend it. It is also an opportunity because firms who are willing to be what customers need in a recession get to keep many of the new customers they get—and cement the loyalty of those they already had.

TAKEAWAYS

Companies tend to cut marketing budgets in a recession. But firms that maintain their marketing spending while reallocating it to suit the new context typically fare better than firms that cut their marketing investment. Examine each of your categories of marketing costs to reflect how well they fit in the new context.

- ✓ **R&D and new product launches.** Research has shown that products launched during a recession have both higher long-term survival chances and higher sales revenues. The best period to launch a new product is just after a recession's midpoint.

- ✓ **Prices and promotions.** Faced with declining sales volume, managers are tempted to increase prices in the hope of maintaining revenues and margins. Avoid seesawing prices.

- ✓ **Communication.** When competitors are cutting back on their brand advertising, your company's share of voice can increase. The content of advertising during recessions must reflect the challenges that consumers are encountering. Consumers in a downturn want to see brands show solidarity.

- ✓ **Tailoring the response to the context.** Companies operating in multiple markets need to choose different strategies for different parts of the business.

NOTES

1. Raji Srinivasan, Arvind Rangaswamy, and Gary L. Lilien, "Turning Adversity into Advantage: Does Proactive Marketing During a Recession Pay Off?" *International Journal of Research in Marketing* 22, vol. 2 (June 2005), https://www.sciencedirect.com/science/article/abs/pii/S0167811605000108.

2. M. Berk Talay, Koen Pauwels, and Steven H. Seggie, "To Launch or Not to Launch in Recessions? Evidence from Over 60 Years of the Automobile Industry," MSI, May 15, 2012, https://www.msi.org/working-papers/to-launch-or-not-to-launch-in-recessions-evidence-from-over-60-years-of-the-automobile-industry/.

3. Raji Srinivasan, Gary L. Lilien, and Shrihari Sridhar, "Should Firms Spend More on Research and Development and Advertising During Recessions?" *Journal of Marketing* 75 (May 2011), https://journals.sagepub.com/doi/abs/10.1509/jmkg.75.3.49?journalCode=jmxa.

4. Koen Pauwels, "Myths on Marketing in Recession," *Smarter Marketing Gets Better Results* (blog), April 10, 2020, https://analyticdashboards.wordpress.com/2020/04/10/myths-on-marketing-in-recession/.

5. "The Game Has Changed," *The Economist*, August 20, 2009, https://www.economist.com/business/2009/08/20/the-game-has-changed.

Adapted from "Don't Cut Your Marketing Budget in a Recession" on hbr.org, August 14, 2020 (product #H05SOY).

7

SEVEN STRATEGIES FOR LEADING A CRISIS-DRIVEN REORG

by Peter Buchas, Stephen Heidari-Robinson, Suzanne Heywood, and Matthias Qian

T he Covid-19 pandemic has forced countless companies to reorganize at an accelerated pace. To understand what makes a crisis-driven reorganization succeed or fail, we drew on our own 15 years of experience advising companies on organizational change as well as a database compiled by Quartz Associates and HBR documenting over 2,500 reorganizations.[1] The database shows that crisis-driven reorganizations are a net benefit in just two-thirds of cases; 19 percent actually damage the company, and only 8 percent fully deliver everything they aim to in the time planned. What can leaders do to increase their chances of success?

Whether a reorganization is motivated by cutting costs or by growth, our research found seven things companies can do to maximize their chances of delivering the intended outcome in the time planned while minimizing disruption.

1. Move Quickly But Always with a Plan.

Time is of the essence. If a crisis-driven reorganization takes longer than six months, it is significantly more likely to fail. After all, the longer it takes, the more likely it is that the business context will have changed (especially in a rapidly developing crisis situation), making the new model irrelevant—something we see in 30 percent of crisis-driven reorgs.

Of course, moving quickly does not mean rushing ahead without a plan. Only a third of companies pursuing a crisis-driven reorg develop a detailed plan; another third have just one milestone that everyone needs to hit; and a final third have no plan whatsoever. The data shows that the latter two cases have much lower success rates. In our HBR Press book, *ReOrg: How to Get It Right*, we go into greater detail on how to successfully plan and implement a reorganization.

2. Analyze Your Human Capital Resources.

The vast majority of companies' human capital analysis capabilities are not nearly as substantial as their financial analysis, leading them to sacrifice either speed or rigor in their reorg. As the HR head of a large U.K. energy company explained, "We do not have the right data on people, so we have to use the blunt instrument approach: I know we need to reduce headcount by a certain amount to cut costs, but I don't really know where the inefficiencies are." Our experience suggests that this situation can be remedied within days or weeks and does not require a multiyear enterprise resource planning implementation.

Nevertheless, rather than investigating their own organizations, some companies attempt to benchmark their cost-saving targets against peer-group companies. This typically takes a long time and results in less reliable comparisons since leaders do not know whether differences are driven by a different context, level of automation, level of outsourcing, or just worse performance. In addition, this sort of analysis is essentially backward-looking, so any conclusions you draw from it may no longer be relevant.

Instead, our data suggests that internal benchmarking analysis (for example, "why is my operations team more efficient in region X than region Y?") is much more likely to lead to success. Internal benchmarking enables companies to move fast, understand what is driving differences, roll out best practices to other areas, and more effectively challenge naysayers with detailed evidence.

3. Set Differentiated Targets and Consider Making Focused Investments.

Saving 20–30 percent across the board is not always the right answer—perhaps some organizational units should be cut by 50, 80, or even 100 percent while others might need focused investment. For example, we once worked with an energy company that had set the same cost-saving target across all departments. They found that some departments, such as HR, remained inefficient even after meeting the new target while others, such as technology, were essentially unable to function after being hollowed out by the reorg. In this case, a differentiated target system would have been better for everyone.

Companies that can reinvest a portion of their cost savings into building up their internal capabilities are significantly more likely to succeed, even if this means cutting costs more deeply elsewhere to afford it. This may be intuitively obvious, but it is easily forgotten in a crisis. For example, when we worked with a logistics company to reduce costs in their quality control department, we found that an existing success framework (and the expensive statisticians who supported it) actually made performance worse. As such, we decided to close down this team and invest some of the savings into growing the department's coaching team that did have a demonstrated record of success.

4. Involve Your Full Leadership Team.

How you decide on organizational change really matters—sometimes even more than the actual decision. The Quartz/HBR data set clearly shows that the most successful reorganizations involve the whole leadership team in the decision-making process, often with some staff input as well. Our experience tells us that this is because the entire leadership team will need to support the execution of the plan, so they all need to buy into it.

Unfortunately, the data shows that this approach is not very common. Instead, crisis-driven reorgs are most frequently designed by just the leader and a few of their most trusted colleagues. This is even worse than a single dictator deciding because executives who feel excluded from the inner leadership circle are more likely to resist later.

5. Allow Some Flexibility in How the New Organizational Model Is Implemented.

In 50 percent of cases, crisis-driven reorgs fail to deliver as planned because leaders resist a centrally mandated solution. Companies that allow leaders some flexibility in deciding how the changes are implemented—ideally based on a solid business rationale—are far more likely to succeed.

For example, when we reorganized a division of an oil and gas company, we agreed that if a geographic business unit was below a certain level of revenue and/or activity, it would not need to make the all the changes that we expected of larger business units but could instead adapt the reorganization design to match its specific circumstances. When we work with companies, we help them to define an overall design, guardrails for what is acceptable, targets for cost, and a process for local leaders to fill in the details. It turns out that this is far quicker and more likely to lead to a workable outcome than deciding on every last detail in advance.

6. Communicate the Changes As Quickly— and Humanely—As Possible.

In everyday reorganizations, face-to-face communication has a much greater correlation with success than communicating via email. However, in crisis-driven reorganizations, electronic communication is actually far more likely to correlate with success—probably because in a fast-moving situation, employees would rather receive news quickly than be left in the dark.

Ultimately, the most important thing for leaders to remember is that reorganizations are not only about numbers—they're also about people. Friends and colleagues will lose their jobs. You have a duty to treat them fairly and sympathetically, and your remaining workforce will judge you on how you handle the situation. Mass, impersonal layoffs by video conference without any forewarning are unlikely to win you accolades from either community.

A better approach is to tell all employees what is happening and why and then to have managers or HR personnel who know the people affected speak to them directly (all of which can be done virtually). Even when changes happen quickly, employees need to understand why, when, and how they will happen.

7. Create a Positive Feedback Loop.

Nancy McKinstry of Wolters Kluwer (rated by HBR as the top-performing female CEO of 2019) told us: "It is unrealistic to expect the new organization to work perfectly from the beginning. You have to live with it and digest it, and rapidly course correct when you find issues." Crisis-driven reorgs that have formal mechanisms for feedback (such as managers escalating issues, staff surveys, or a formal review three to six months after completion) are much more likely to be successful while reorgs without clear processes for escalating issues are most likely to fail.

Interestingly, while growth-driven reorgs consistently benefit from surveying employees about implementation issues, our research suggests that this approach is less effective for cost-cutting reorgs. This may be because cost-cutting is by nature divisive, so staff may take longer to embrace the changes and contribute positively rather than focus on their concerns. Nonetheless, companies which have completed a cost-cutting reorg should not neglect other formal means of assessing organizational performance post-launch.

Delivering organizational change in a crisis is never easy, and Covid-19 poses unprecedented challenges. But armed with the seven guidelines listed above, you are much more likely to succeed.

The Covid-19 pandemic and subsequent recession have forced countless companies to reorganize at an accelerated pace, yet only 8 percent of crisis-driven reorganizations deliver as planned. Companies looking to reorganize in response to a crisis should follow these seven strategies.

✓ **Move quickly, but always with a plan.** The longer it takes, the more likely it is that the business context will have changed.

✓ **Analyze your human capital resources.** Internal benchmarking analysis is more likely to lead to success than benchmarking against peer-group companies.

✓ **Set differentiated targets and consider making focused investment.** Reinvest a portion of your cost savings into building up their internal capabilities.

✓ **Involve your full leadership team.** The entire leadership team will need to support the execution of the plan, so they all need to be bought into it.

✓ **Allow some flexibility in how the new organizational model is implemented.** Companies that allow leaders some flexibility—based on a solid business rationale— are far more likely to succeed.

✓ **Communicate the changes as quickly—and humanely—as possible.** Tell all employees what is happening and why, and then have managers or HR personnel who know the people affected speak to them directly.

✓ **Create a positive feedback loop.** Include formal mechanisms and clear processes for employee feedback about the reorg.

NOTE

1. Stephen Heidari-Robinson and Suzanne Heywood, "Assessment: How Successful Was Your Company's Reorg?" hbr.org, February 24, 2017, https://hbr.org/2017/02/assessment-how-successful-was-your -companys-reorg.

Adapted from "7 Strategies for Leading a Crisis-Driven Reorg" on hbr.org, August 31, 2020 (product #H05TUN).

Section 3

ENTREPRENEURSHIP AND STARTUPS IN THE RECESSION

8

YOU DON'T HAVE TO PIVOT IN A CRISIS

by Daniel Isenberg and Alessandro Di Fiore

When Covid-19 burst upon the scene in early 2020, startup ventures faced dramatic shifts in markets, and the importance of strategic agility became axiomatic: If you wanted your venture to survive, let alone thrive, pundits (including ourselves) almost universally advocated deep internal cuts accompanied by pivots to new markets and business models.[1] As the leadership of the tech-focused California venture capital firm Sequoia Capital wrote in a March *Medium* post identifying Covid-19 as the black swan of 2020, "Nobody ever regrets making fast and decisive adjustments to changing circumstances."[2]

However, ventures we know well through our investment portfolio (Isenberg is a minor [< 1 percent] shareholder in Guesty, X24 Factory, and Camp) and network—many well-funded startups in hard-hit industries such as hospitality, travel, and furniture shunned strategic agility (changing product-market fit) for stability and resolutely stayed the course with only minor tweaks. Examples include:

- TravelPerk, a Barcelona-based online provider of corporate travel services, which has raised $140 million in seed and expansion capital

- X24 Factory, a Berlin-based operator of online European home furniture marketplaces, which has raised $13 million from private and fund investors in Europe

- Guesty, a Tel Aviv–based global platform that automates and streamlines the daily operational tasks for short-term rental management companies listing on Airbnb and the like, which has raised over $60 million since graduating from Y Combinator in 2014

Despite the turmoil in their markets, TravelPerk, X24 Factory, and Guesty all made the conscious decision to *not* pivot and deliberately maintained their strategies, their business models, and their teams with only marginal changes. However, staying the course doesn't mean inaction. Across the observed portfolio of ventures, we found some commonalities, a set of rules that the "stay-the-course" companies followed: slow down, reaffirm your thesis, trim around the edges, watch the data, and test for weakness—and if you do have to pivot, do it explosively.

Immediately slow down. Entrepreneurs tend to run at breakneck speed—these companies were no exception. However, when their markets started to melt down, rather than slamming on the brakes, they downshifted to listen to customers, track the market, conserve resources, and enhance their ability to change direction *if needed*.

There is an analogy in the animal world: the cheetah, the world's fastest land animal, pursues its prey at just *half* speed, rarely reaching even close to its 70 miles per hour limit. Scientists believe that this strategy allows the cheetah to save its strength and preserve optionality by not overcommitting to a wrong direction when its prey suddenly shifts.

These companies followed a similar logic. As Avi Meir, co-founding CEO of TravelPerk, put it, "We slowed down decision making because it was a wartime scenario with little information, and the worst thing would have been to run amuck." Meir wanted to keep his and his team's eyes sharply focused on TravelPerk's long-term vision and avoid making rash decisions that might compromise that vision.

Take time to reaffirm your basic thesis. Slowing down also allowed these entrepreneurs to make double sure that their view of their future marketplace was still valid.

Amiad Soto, co-founding CEO of Guesty, engaged his board and executive team to look a few months out; he concluded that Guesty's fundamentals had not changed one bit: "During the pandemic, people still seek vacation rentals, even though the specific patterns might change: In addition to cleanliness and safety being paramount, we concluded that vacation and short term rentals would become longer and demand would increase. We are in the business of helping/ensuring property management companies thrive, and that did not change for us," reflected Soto.

Meir saw additional benefits to TravelPerk staying true to its initial vision: "We saw our better-resourced competitors acting too fast." As competitors rushed into major layoffs, TravelPerk picked up many of their corporate customers "because we kept our sales and service capacity intact while they rashly cut costs," commented Meir. Meir felt comfortable continuing to invest in staff because he was confident that the company's core thesis remained the same.

Trim fat, not muscle. Part of slowing down is trimming operations, but only around the margins. This is counter to the now-conventional wisdom of crisis-driven cutting into the muscle by reducing payroll faster and deeper than you think is necessary. Yes, take advantage of the fall in prices to renegotiate rental leases and supplier contracts, but consider making only marginal cuts in payroll expenses, primarily through performance management rather than layoffs or furloughs. As Meir reflected, "We cut fat, not muscle or bone like our competitors," preserving TravelPerk's strength and flexibility.

Watch new data like a hawk. Within days of the lockdowns starting, X24 Factory saw demand for furniture plummet by 40 percent, according to founding CEO Miro Morczinek. "But rather than overreact, we first started looking at all kinds of new data. We looked at Italy to see how their worst-case scenario might apply to our major market in Germany. We looked at job searches to see where the layoffs were happening in our supply chain. We studied other verticals such as cars and travel to see how they were being impacted." At first, this seemed to Morczinek like a replay of the 2008 recession, but after setting up an hourly data watch, "On the second weekend after lockdown, our intense monitoring showed a surprising explosion in demand." It emerged that the lockdown was allowing people to accelerate home improvement projects and pushing them to move living space outdoors, with garden furniture more than compensated for losses in other categories, and in response, "We only tweaked our messaging."

Test for weaknesses and prepare internally. Companies should apply increased scrutiny not only to the marketplace but also to their own internal points of failure. You can stay the course only if you stay ahead of the organizational disruption that external shocks can cause. "On March 11, I conducted a surprise 'fire drill' by requiring everyone to work from home in order to learn what our weaknesses were," recalled TravelPerk's Meir. Remote work was unprecedented at the venture, and they quickly identified problems—home offices with no air conditioning so windows had to stay open to noisy streets below, poor internet connections, and the lack of desk chairs. Meir created a team to resolve these issues and completed equipping 500 home offices on the weekend Spain locked down the entire country.

If and when you do pivot, consider doing it explosively. Back to our cheetah. In addition to holding the mammalian speed record, the cheetah is also the champion of redirecting its body—they change speed and direction better than trained polo horses and accelerate faster than race-track greyhounds. When a cheetah does change direction, it does so with unparalleled decisiveness and commitment, digging its nonretractable claws in while wrenching its lithe physique toward its prey.

In-store retailers have been crushed by Covid-19, but Ben Kaufman, co-founding CEO of the retail family experience startup Camp, pivoted like a cheetah. Anticipating in February that sheltering-in-place would soon reach the United States, by mid-March Kaufman had shuttered all five of Camp's new, high-end "family experience stores" and furloughed 130 retail staff. Following just days of intense discussions, Kaufman and Amanda Raposo, Camp's chief experience officer, started bringing their entire in-store family experience into the home, first launching Camp's Zoom birthday parties, which within a few months were contributing (along with other new digital products) to the revenues that surpassed pre-pandemic forecasts. Camp went on to cut major deals with Walmart and other retailers to imbue their brands with Camp's unique online family engagement.

Methodically not-pivoting can pay off—in the right situation, that is. Staying the course, with minor adjustments, has proved to be a winning strategy for these ventures: "For the first time since founding, X24 Factory is significantly profitable," commented X24 Factory's

Morczinek. TravelPerk is adding new customers and winning market share and in fact exceeded its July forecast by 100 percent. Guesty is seeing significant increases in longer-term rentals. The lesson here is that when a crisis hits, it pays to resist knee-jerk reactions on how to handle external shocks and to ask what is going to work best for your company, based on the particular realities of its business. Ignoring the playbook of rapid cuts plus strategic pivoting can be the smart move.

TAKEAWAYS

Not every startup up venture should follow the conventional wisdom to pivot quickly in a crisis. Startups that "stay the course" can follow a set of rules to improve their likelihood of success.

- ✓ **Immediately slow down.** Downshift in order to listen to customers, track the market, conserve resources, and enhance your ability to change direction *if needed.*

- ✓ **Take time to reaffirm your basic thesis.** Make double sure that your views of the future marketplace are still valid.

✓ **Trim fat, not muscle.** Cut operating costs, but only around the margins. Consider making only marginal cuts in payroll expenses, primarily through performance management.

✓ **Watch new data like a hawk.** Seek out new types of data wherever possible.

✓ **Test for weaknesses and prepare internally.** Apply increased scrutiny not only to the marketplace but also to your own internal points of failure.

✓ **If and when you do pivot, pivot explosively.** If you change direction, do so with decisiveness and commitment.

NOTES

1. Daniel Isenberg and Alessandro Di Fiore, "Entrepreneurs: How to Change Your Business Model in the Pandemic," *LSE Business Review*, May 8, 2020, https://blogs.lse.ac.uk/businessreview/2020/05/08/entrepreneurs-how-to-change-your-business-model-in-the-pandemic/.

2. Sequoia Capital, "Coronavirus: The Black Swan of 2020," *Medium*, March 5, 2020, https://medium.com/sequoia-capital/coronavirus-the-black-swan-of-2020-7c72bdeb9753.

Adapted from "You Don't Have to Pivot in a Crisis" on hbr.org, September 21, 2020 (product #H05VFL).

9

HOW TO LAUNCH A STARTUP IN THE POST-COVID ERA

by Uri Adoni

A look back at history shows us that crises are opportune moments for new ideas, innovations, and systems. Some of the most famous companies today were launched right after the 2008 economic crisis: WhatsApp, Uber, Slack, AirBnb, and Groupon, etc. are a few noteworthy examples.

This economic crisis due to the coronavirus pandemic can feel challenging and terrifying, but the current environment can be an ambitious time for young entrepreneurs to launch the startup of their dreams.

Pitching an idea and raising capital for your startup may be harder than before, but understanding the market and the needs of the consumer (as well as your own adaptability during a crisis) can help you stay in the game.

Here are several practical tips for both existing startups and new startups that are planning to fundraise in the next six to 12 months.

Be brutally honest—what makes sense *now*? Ask yourself: Have the recent global events changed the relevancy of my product and proposition? Does my idea still answer the same needs as before? Does the offering need to be updated based on the new reality? Are there any changes or adaptations to be made on the product, offering, technology, pricing, distribution channels, or the geographies I'm targeting?

Answer these questions honestly. A crisis will likely decrease certain market needs and increase others. Make adjustments to meet the new market needs and conditions. For example, Athena Security makes software that allows security cameras to detect firearms in real-time. Now, with Covid-19, they are selling systems that use thermal cameras to detect a person with a fever in real-time. Room, a startup that makes phone booths as a quiet refuge in open-plan offices, is now making coronavirus-testing booths for healthcare clinics.

Understand how the needs of the market and the consumer have changed, and innovate your startup or new idea. Think about how you want to be relevant NOW.

Understand the mindset of the investors you meet. Generally, there are investors who are more conservative, and in times of a crisis they tend to hold their cash and pause their investments, while others are more adventurous and look for great opportunities with lower valuations. Try to assess which of the two is the potential investor you're meeting. If the meeting is with a venture capital firm, you should find out when the fund was launched to determine where they are on their cash deployments. For younger funds that are only one or two years old, they will be actively looking to invest, and the crisis could be a great time to invest because the valuations of most companies will drop. However, many of those funds will also want to mitigate the risk by investing in more mature companies that have a clear path to profitability. As you will do on normal days, you should also make sure that the VC you are meeting has an interest in the space you are active in and has made an investment in this vertical before.

Think like a camel, not like a unicorn. Camels are built for survival in some of the toughest climates on earth. They are resilient and can survive for many weeks without food or water, still running fast when needed. On the other hand, the mythical unicorns in the business world are focused on rapid growth through deep funding and an accessible talent pool.

A crisis is a time for demonstrating camel behavior. The vast majority of startups have an ambitious vision, with big plans and large numbers. This is fine and shouldn't be changed. But during a crisis, everyone is cash-sensitive, and you should be too. Be cash flow-sensitive, have a lean organization, create a realistic and conservative operational budget, and make sure you don't deviate from it. Possible investors will want to see that you manage your cash cautiously and wisely, don't make any long-term financial commitments, and know-how to cut expenses when needed.

Be open and transparent with your investors. Make sure investors are fully aware of your company's situation, changes that occurred in the market you are operating in, challenges you are facing, updated projections for revenues, and a list of realistic needs for short-term and future funding.

Explain how you have addressed the challenges—this could give them important insight into how you function when times get tough and the decision-making process within the company. Don't sugarcoat things. Treat your investors as part of your team.

Build a strong advisory board. This is true to any startup at any time, but during crisis times, this is of utmost importance. Having experienced people who can assist you in running and growing your venture will also give more confidence to investors. They will know that even if you are a first-time entrepreneur, you have veteran business-people to guide and assist you when needed. In addition, this advisory board can use their own networks to make introductions and open relevant doors at times when opportunities are scanty.

Be ready for post-crisis growth. Ensure that you have a full operational plan ready for the day after when things get back to normal. Make sure the business plan reflects how you'll adapt when the skies clear up and grow your business.

Economic downturns, although challenging, can provide an opportunity for launching new companies and products. Crises are opportune moments for new ideas, innovations, and systems. The following advice can help both new and existing startups.

- ✓ **Be brutally honest—what makes sense *now*?** Does your idea still answer the same needs as before? Does the offering need to be updated based on the new reality?

- ✓ **Understand the mindset of the investors you meet.** Times of crisis make some investors more conservative and others more adventurous. Try to assess which of the two the potential investor you're meeting is.

- ✓ **Think like a camel, not like a unicorn.** Have a lean organization, create a realistic and conservative operational budget, and make sure you don't deviate from it. Possible investors will want to see that you manage your cash cautiously and wisely.

- ✓ **Be open and transparent with your investors.** Make sure investors are fully aware of your company's situation. Explain how you have addressed the challenges—this could give them important insight into how you function when times get tough.

- ✓ **Build a strong advisory board.** Having experienced people who can assist you in running and growing your venture will also give more confidence to investors.

✓ **Be ready for post-crisis growth.** Ensure that you have a full operational plan ready for the day after when things get back to normal.

Adapted from "How to Launch a Startup in the Post-Covid Era" on hbr.org (product #H05RVF).

Section 4

MANAGING YOURSELF AND YOUR CAREER IN THE RECESSION

HOW TO FIND A (GREAT) JOB DURING A DOWNTURN

by Claudio Fernández-Aráoz

U nemployment rates have spiked around the world owing to the Covid-19 crisis and its economic fall-out. The landmark research on how people find good jobs was conducted in the early 1970s by Mark Granovetter and remains relevant today despite the big changes in roles and recruitment that we've seen since.[1] Studying professional, technical, and managerial job seekers, Granovetter found that most jobs (and especially good ones) were attained not through direct application or other formal means—that is, submitting a resume in response to a listing (which then might have been a print ad but is now online)—but through "personal contacts," who told the applicant about the position or recommended them to someone inside the organization.

Job seekers preferred this approach, noting that they got (and were able to give) better information during the process. Those who secured employment also benefited from higher pay on average and were more likely to be "very satisfied" in their roles, some of which, they reported, were even custom-created to suit their skills, knowledge, and experience. Based on more than 30 years of executive search experience, I'm convinced that most employers also prefer to work this way.

It's critical to understand which of your personal contacts are the most useful though. Granovetter also found that you're more likely to find jobs through personal contacts who are *not* too close to you, speak to you infrequently, and work in occupations different than your own. He captured this notion in a wonderful expression— "the strength of weak ties"—and many other researchers have since confirmed that diverse personal networks are the best way to find a new job. These acquaintances might come from your neighborhood, college, high school, fraternal organizations or sports teams, recreational or hobby groups; they might even be people you met once on vacation. In my view, activating these connections is the *only* job-seeking strategy that will allow you to secure a *great* position in truly tough times like the ones we're now enduring, and you must go about it in a disciplined way. Here's how.

Creating Your Contact List

During my first 20 years as a search consultant, I tried to find time each day to help one person who was either without a job or keen for a new one. This made for some 4,000 meetings with job seekers, many of which I conducted in Argentina, as its economy was in deep turmoil. In 2001, for example, it suffered the largest sovereign debt default in world history, and annualized gross domestic product fell by 30 percent coupled with a 300 percent currency devaluation. My advice during those daunting days: Come up with a list of 100 (yes, *one hundred!*) weak ties without making any contact. The rationale? First, simple statistics: The probability of any one person leading you to the perfect job will be very low, so you have to tap many to improve your odds. Second and even more important: Because of the "weak" nature of these contacts, it won't be immediately obvious who can be most helpful. When you work to expand the list, you add quite unexpected people, including some truly great ones. Natural candidates for your weak ties list include former bosses, colleagues and professors, consultants, lawyers, auditors, suppliers, clients, and so on. Some will be potential employers; others, sources. Look for ties in sectors that are likely to be stronger than most in the coming years and that you would really like to work in.

Next, rank everyone you've listed based on two factors: the attractiveness of the possibilities they can offer (given their company, role, and connections) and their willingness to help you (which depends on the quality of your relationship, even if it was limited or distant).

Making Connections

You might assume that I would tell you to make first contact with the person at the very top of the list. But I won't. Instead, start with number 10 or so. You will be nervous, tight, even shy at the beginning, and you will make mistakes. So gain confidence with a few lower-stakes conversations, and then start contacting your most promising targets. Make sure to rapidly cover the top 30 or so, ideally within a period of no more than a week or two. (If you're lucky enough to find more than one possibility, it would be ideal to consider all of them at once.)

Of course, each conversation will be different depending on the person, opportunity, and previous relationship. But, with everyone, be candid about your reason for calling, the type of role you're looking for, and what you have to offer. People who have had a positive experience working with you will most likely want to help you, but they can't if they are unaware of or unclear on your need and aspirations.

Closing the List

In deciding when to end this process, you can make two types of mistakes: If you contact too few ties, you might not find any opportunities. If you contact too many, you might waste precious time on less attractive possibilities which will prevent you from properly focusing on the best ones. The key is to stop the calls when you have enough leads to give you a significant chance of landing a job. Consider, for example, that, as a result of your disciplined list-making and contact process, you are down to three potential employers. You estimate you have a 50 percent shot at getting the first job, 40 percent for the second, and 30 percent for the third. The probability of getting at least one offer can be easily calculated as one minus the product of the complementary probabilities, or $1 - (0.5 \times 0.6 \times 0.7) = 79$ percent. If you'd prefer to be 90 percent certain of getting a job, you'll need to keep calling prospects.

How do you go about estimating these probabilities? Simply use your judgment. If you were one out of three finalists in a search, your chances of landing that job would be one-third, or 33 percent. On the other hand, some leads might be so weak that only one out of 50 would turn into an offer, a probability of 2 percent. You should not eliminate these cases at this stage, though! If you contact 100 prospects with a 2 percent individual chance, the probability of getting at least one offer comes out at 87 percent, since $1 - 0.98^{100} = 87$ percent.

Make your best estimate in each case, and don't worry too much about precision at this stage. Once you start getting answers (or not) from each of your contacts, these probabilities will start moving up (when there's mutual interest) or down. In the end most of them will turn to zero while just a few will become significant. I've developed a downloadable support tool to help you track this.[2]

Managing Leads

At this point, you will hopefully have several leads. To keep all those balls in the air, even as you reach out to more of your targets, you'll need to proactively follow-up on every promising conversation, including contacting new people that your weak ties have recommended you try. This can feel daunting! But, again, the support tool can help. It is a fully automated Excel spreadsheet, which includes a series of intuitive macro commands to easily sort leads by name, status (sources or potential employers), company, pending actions and deadlines, probability of receiving an offer, and priority. It will also automatically calculate the compounded probability of getting at least one offer so that you can more objectively decide when to move from lead generation to closure.

Sealing the Deal

As you talk to potential employers, you'll of course want to follow all standard job-seeking advice. Before you share your resume, make sure that you have updated it and that it stands out. When interviewing—which at this stage is likely to happen virtually—refresh yourself on best practices. Be able to answer open-ended prompts or behavioral prompts like, "So tell me about yourself" or "Tell me about a time when you overcame conflict/led a large team/had to collaborate across silos/managed a change initiative." Prepare and practice, including finding a quiet room with good lighting, and keep in mind the special challenges of virtual interviewing.

Remember to think carefully about your own priorities, preferences, and broader purpose and match them up against all the opportunities. Keep updating the spreadsheet with probabilities and new to-dos as the discussions progress. For your top priorities, create a strong list of references and let those people know that employers might be calling about you. Research the organization and its target markets. And, as venture capitalist Jeff Bussgang advises, come bearing gifts, such as proposals or project help, that show your commitment and work product.

A Composite Case Study

Let's consider the case of Juana, a character I've drawn from several professionals with whom I've worked. Born in the United States to working-class parents who emigrated from Mexico, she got her first job while in high school, working at a well-known fast food franchise. By 19, she was the manager of a restaurant and was pursuing her bachelor's degree in accounting. After graduation, she joined a Big Three consulting firm, earned her CPA, and rapidly advanced from analyst to manager in a few years. In November 2019, she accepted an offer from

JOB SEARCH TOOL

							P (At Least 1 Offer) =	55%

Sort		Sort	Sort	Sort		Sort		Sort	Sort	Sort
35		0	0	0	35	0	0	35	0	35
LAST NAME	**NAME**	**PRIORITY**	**NEXT ACTION**	**DEADLINE**	**CONTACT**	**INTERVIEW**	**SOURCE**	**COMPANY**	**EMPLOYER**	**P(Offer)**
Jones	Peter				1-Feb-21			eretail Startup		10%
Camara	Joao				1-Feb-21			College		5%
Hubler	Eric				1-Feb-21			Former Client		5%
Westley	Casey				1-Feb-21			Consulting Firm		5%
Gunninghan	John				1-Feb-21			Consulting Firm		2%
Miles	Fiona				1-Feb-21			College		2%
O'Brian	Caroline				1-Feb-21			Consulting Firm		2%
Other	Other				1-Feb-21			College		2%
Other	Other				1-Feb-21			College		2%
Other	Other				1-Feb-21			College		2%
Other	Other				1-Feb-21			College		2%
Other	Other				1-Feb-21			College		2%
Other	Other				1-Feb-21			College		2%
Other	Other				1-Feb-21			Fast Food Franch.		2%
Other	Other				1-Feb-21			Fast Food Franch.		2%
Other	Other				1-Feb-21			Former Client		2%
Other	Other				1-Feb-21			Former Client		2%
Other	Other				1-Feb-21			Former Client		2%
Other	Other				1-Feb-21			Uncle		2%

one of her clients, a global hotel chain, to join the company and lead its global HR analytics projects. Then the Covid-19 crisis hit. Juana's project was canceled, and on March 31, she was laid off. As a mother to two little girls, sharing responsibility for a mortgage and aging parents with her husband, she needed a new job. She spent the next week compiling a list of contacts. On April 5, she sent 35 emails to the most obvious sources and potential employers: a few managers and colleagues from the consulting firm, some former professors, an uncle, and several college classmates. She estimated that her probability of getting an offer from each ranged from 10 percent for her most recent boss at the consulting firm to 2 percent for most of the contacts. As can be seen in the previous screen capture, the compounded probability of getting at least one offer from this first group was just 55 percent.

So, on April 10, Juana emailed 30 more people on her list, including several former bosses from the fast food franchise, all her former clients at the consulting firm, and a few additional personal connections. That increased her compounded probability of getting at least one offer to 78 percent. But that wasn't enough for Juana! On April 15, she sent six more emails, including one to Pablo Rodríguez, a former HR leader for Latin America at the fast food company, who she had met just once at the company's worldwide convention when she won an award for best restaurant managers. While Juana received no response from most of the 71 contacts she emailed, a dozen replied, including a former manager who was interested in her joining his electronic retail startup (to which she assigned a 40 percent probability of getting an offer), another manager who was interested in bringing her back (35 percent chance), and three other significant leads.

By April 18, less than three weeks after being fired, the top of Juana's process spreadsheet can be seen on p. 118.

Having reached a compounded probability of 93 percent of getting a job, Juana decided it was time to move from lead generation to closure. On page 119 you can see that she sorted the opportunities by priority rather than probability.

The job she thought she'd be most likely to get, a role at the electronic retail startup, was attractive because of her experience working with its founder and its potential financial upside; however, it would be a risky venture, with long and demanding hours. A job at her former consulting firm was second most likely to come to fruition. She liked the company and her colleagues, but its policy was to put her back into her previous role at the same pay and she wasn't sure she wanted to return to consulting work.

At the top of her ranking, surprisingly, was an alternative generated by Pablo Rodríguez, who had left the fast

JOB SEARCH TOOL

P (At Least 1 Offer) = 93%

Sort 35	Sort	Sort 8	Sort 8	Sort 8	35	3	Sort 0	Sort 35	Sort 10	Sort 35
LAST NAME	NAME	PRIORITY	NEXT ACTION	DEADLINE	CONTACT	INTERVIEW	SOURCE	COMPANY	EMPLOYER	P(Offer)
Jones	Peter	4	Discussion Pay	25-Feb-21	1-Feb-21	15-Feb-21		eretail Startup	1	40%
Smith	Brenda	3	Final Interview	1-Mar-21	1-Feb-21	24-Feb-21		Consulting Firm	1	35%
Rodriguez	Pablo	1	Deep Discussion	5-Mar-21	5-Feb-21	18-Feb-21		College	1	30%
Hubler	Eric	4	Discussion	5-Mar-21	1-Feb-21			Former Client	1	25%
Camara	Joao	5	Check Location	10-Mar-21	1-Feb-21			College	1	20%
Shakespeare	Joanna	3	Check Business	15-Mar-21	1-Feb-21			College	1	10%
Robbins	Sarah	2	Meet Partners	1-Mar-21	1-Feb-21			College	1	10%
Westley	Casey	2	Deep Zoom Call	20-Mar-21	1-Feb-21			Consulting Firm	1	5%
Wood	George	6			1-Feb-21			College	1	5%
Vasudeva	Sanjiv	6			1-Feb-21			Consulting Firm	1	5%
Gunningham	John	6			1-Feb-21			Consulting Firm		2%
Miles	Fiona	6			1-Feb-21			College		2%
O'Brian	Caroline	6			1-Feb-21			Consulting Firm		2%

JOB SEARCH TOOL

| | | | | | | | | P (At Least 1 Offer) = | | 93% |

Sort		Sort	Sort	Sort			Sort	Sort	Sort	Sort
35		8	8	8	35	3	0	35	10	35
LAST NAME	NAME	PRIORITY	NEXT ACTION	DEADLINE	CONTACT	INTERVIEW	SOURCE	COMPANY	EMPLOYER	P(Offer)
Rodriguez	Pablo	1	Deep Discussion	5-Mar-21	5-Feb-21	18-Feb-21		College	1	30%
Robbins	Sarah	2	Meet Partners	1-Mar-21	1-Feb-21			College	1	10%
Westley	Casey	2	Deep Zoom Call	20-Mar-21	1-Feb-21			Consulting Firm	1	5%
Smith	Brenda	3	Final Interview	1-Mar-21	1-Feb-21	24-Feb-21		Consulting Firm	1	35%
Shakespeare	Joanna	3	Check Business	15-Mar-21	1-Feb-21			College	1	10%
Jones	Peter	4	Discussion Pay	25-Feb-21	1-Feb-21	15-Feb-21		eretail Startup	1	40%
Hubler	Eric	4	Discussion	5-Mar-21	1-Feb-21			Former Client	1	25%
Camara	Joao	5	Check Location	10-Mar-21	1-Feb-21			College	1	20%

food chain a few years earlier to join a 15-year-old, rapidly expanding foundation with the purpose of helping poor, young high school graduates from Latin America to prepare for, access, and persevere in quality jobs. He thought Juana could help him lead a digital transformation that would allow the organization to access a much larger population, including to the U.S. Latino population, at a fraction of the cost. The role would pay less than the others but would allow her to work from home, reconnect with her roots, and give back to the Latin American community.

Confirming her strong interest in that job, Juana had several Zoom discussions with Pablo and the foundation's CEO and founder, did her own research on the needs of the young poor in Latin America and the U.S. Latino population, and prepared a detailed digital transformation plan. Her final interview was on April 20, and she nailed it. Less than three weeks after losing her job, she had a new one she could not feel more passionate about.

Better Opportunities

The dramatic economic, social, and even geopolitical crisis we are going through has only started. It will be deep, long, and far-reaching.

Despite the awful job market, today's practical conditions for exploring new jobs have actually improved. Most people can—and will expect to—interview you virtually. If you're employed and working from home, you'll be able to conduct as many interviews as you can generate without explaining why you need to be away from the office. If you are unemployed, you'll probably be able to consider roles across geographies now that remote work has become commonplace. The lockdowns have also blessed us with an exceptional chance for deep reflection and reassessment of what matters most in life. We can creatively redefine our own identities, aiming toward better and happier versions of ourselves. This could be an opportunity to find a great job more suited to your talents, purpose, and ambitions. If you follow the process above, this is not only possible but highly likely. It has helped the thousands of people I've advised through good times and bad, and I sincerely hope it also works beautifully for you!

TAKEAWAYS

For those seeking jobs during the current health and economic crisis, the outlook might seem bleak. However, by approaching your search in a disciplined way, you can drastically increase your chances of success.

✓ Create a list of 100 potential contacts. This large number is recommended as the odds of any one person leading to the perfect job are low, but in aggregate they are greater.

✓ When you reach out, be candid about your reason for calling, the type of role you're looking for, and what you have to offer. They can't help you if they are unaware of or unclear on your need and aspirations.

✓ Track and prioritize leads as well as their probability of leading you to a good job.

✓ Seal the deal by practicing and preparing for the special challenges of virtual interviewing.

NOTES

1. Marc Miller, "To Get a Job, Use Your Weak Ties," *Forbes*, August 17, 2016, https://www.forbes.com/sites/nextavenue/2016/08 /17/to-get-a-job-use-your-weak-ties/#2deb7b886b87.

2. You can download the support tool at https://hbr.org/resources/ pdfs/hbr-articles/2020/FernandezAraoz_JOB_SEARCH_TOOL.xlsm.

Adapted from "How to Find a (Great) Job During a Pandemic" on hbr.org, June 15, 2020 (product #H05OA4).

11

GROWTH AFTER TRAUMA

by Richard G. Tedeschi

What good can come of this? In times of stress, crisis, or trauma, people often ask that question. This year we've been hit by a pandemic that has caused hundreds of thousands of deaths, unprecedented unemployment, and a global economic downturn. In the face of such a tragedy—personal and collective—it might appear that the answer is "Nothing."

However, at some point we will be able to reflect on the long-term consequences of this terrible time and what it has wrought for each of us as individuals and for our organizations, communities, and nations. Almost certainly those outcomes will include some good along with the bad. Over the past 25 years psychologists like me have been studying this phenomenon. We refer to it as *posttraumatic growth.*

We've learned that negative experiences can spur positive change, including a recognition of personal strength, the exploration of new possibilities, improved relationships, a greater appreciation for life, and spiritual growth. We see this in people who have endured war, natural disasters, bereavement, job loss and economic stress, serious illnesses and injuries. So despite the misery resulting from the coronavirus outbreak, many of us can expect to develop in beneficial ways in its aftermath. And leaders can help others to do so.

Although posttraumatic growth often happens naturally, without psychotherapy or other formal intervention, it can be facilitated in five ways: through education, emotional regulation, disclosure, narrative development, and service. As a researcher and a practicing psychotherapist, I (and my colleagues) have helped hundreds of people emerge stronger from suffering in these ways. You can emerge stronger yourself. And you can serve as what we call an *expert companion* for others, encouraging introspection and curiosity, actively listening, and offering compassionate feedback.

The Elements of Growth

Here are the five ways in more detail.

Education.

To move through trauma to growth, one must first get educated about what the former is: a disruption of core belief systems. For example, before the pandemic, many of us thought we were safe from the types of diseases that endangered people in the past; that bad things happened in other parts of the world but not ours; and that our social and economic systems were resilient enough to weather all storms. None of that was true. So now we need to figure out what to believe instead.

When our assumptions are challenged, it is confusing and frightening and tends to produce anxious, repetitive thinking: *Why did this happen? Who's in control? What should I do now?* We are forced to rethink who we are, what kind of people surround us, what world we live in, and what future we will have. It can be extremely painful. But as research shows, it can also usher in change that will be of value. We must begin by learning and understanding that truth.

I once counseled a woman who, in her thirties, was disabled by a stroke and initially struggled to cope. But she soon understood that her changed circumstances would require her to reevaluate her identity: "Now I have to figure out what is next in this life I never thought I would be living. Part of me doesn't want to think I have to do this, but I know I do." That was the first step in her becoming a person with more compassion for herself who could accept limitations without being limited by them.

As we move through the current health and economic crisis, consider how you can reinforce—to yourself and others—the recognition that it may have a positive as well as a negative impact. Remember that you and others in your team and organization can reimagine how you operate and innovate in new circumstances. That may already be evident in the emergency measures taken to keep things going. For example, I know an IT employee of a food service company that laid off most of its workers earlier this year. As one of the few to remain, she was forced to work in functions and areas she'd never touched before, which was a struggle. But she soon realized that unencumbered by the usual bureaucracy and turf battles, she could ferret out inefficiencies and find ways to improve on old procedures.

Emotional regulation.

To do any learning, one must be in the right frame of mind. That starts with managing negative emotions such as anxiety, guilt, and anger, which can be done by shifting the kind of thinking that leads to those feelings. Instead of focusing on losses, failures, uncertainties, and worst-case scenarios, try to recall successes, consider best-case possibilities, reflect on your own or your organization's resources and preparation, and think reasonably about what you—personally and as a group—can do.

For the founder of one dining chain, emotional regulation was crucial after Michael Mack's board ousted him from the CEO role. As reported in HBR ("Crucible: Losing the Top Job—and Winning It Back," October 2010), the news came as a complete shock, and he was furious at first. But when his father, also an investor, told him to "get [his] head around being supportive," he did. Instead of focusing on his anger and the feeling that he'd been betrayed, he started thinking about how he could stay calm and professional and help the business going forward. He eventually returned to lead the company.

You can regulate emotions directly by observing them as they are experienced. Physical exercise and meditative practices such as breathing also help. Employ these techniques yourself, and share them to help others. Acknowledge that circumstances continue to be both challenging and frightening, then demonstrate poise under that pressure. And encourage more-frequent communication so that people feel less isolated and see their collective emotional strength more clearly.

Disclosure.

This is the part of the process in which you talk about what has happened and is happening: its effects—both small and broad, short- and long-term, personal and professional, individual and organizational—and what you are struggling with in its wake. Articulating these things helps us to make sense of the trauma and turn debilitating thoughts into more-productive reflections.

If you're helping someone talk about what it's been like to experience this crisis, asking a lot of questions can seem like an intrusive interrogation spurred by curiosity rather than concern. It's best to focus on how the impact feels and which of your counterpart's concerns are most important.

A case study comes from a former client. A talented developer getting established in a new company, he created a program that had great promise. But then his bosses hired someone from the outside to run it, asking my client to report to him. Led by this manager, the program under-performed, and the developer was being blamed, damaging his reputation and career prospects. Finally he went to HR. "I wasn't sure if this was the right move," he told me, "but I needed to get some advice." Talking to the HR representative was cathartic, and he ended up telling her more than he'd planned to because she asked questions such as "What did it feel like to have this project taken from you and essentially messed up?" She then worked to help him recover from that big professional setback.

It is important for you as a colleague and a leader to understand the varying impacts the pandemic and the ensuing market volatility, layoffs, and recession have had and continue to have on the lives of those around you. Start by speaking openly about your own struggles and how you are managing the uncertainty. You can then invite others to tell their stories and listen attentively as they locate their difficulties and come to terms with how their challenges and losses compare with those of others.

Narrative development.

The next step is to produce an authentic narrative about the trauma and our lives afterward so that we can accept the chapters already written and imagine crafting the next ones in a meaningful way. Your story—and the stories of people you're helping—can and should be about a traumatic past that leads to a better future.

Consider a nonprofit executive who had been fired from two previous positions over sexual harassment allegations. One night, as he and his wife were driving on the interstate, they were involved in a horrific crash, plowing into a stopped vehicle that didn't have its lights on. His wife's injuries were minor, but he was left comatose for a month and needed a year of rehabilitation to walk and talk again. His new narrative went something like this: "Many would think it was this accident that put my life in jeopardy. But I was already in great danger. I was causing pain to others, ruining my career, and heading for a life without my wife or children. The accident forced me to stop, created time for reflection, and showed me what love really is."

When you're ready, start to shape the narrative of this year's trauma for yourself and your organization. How has it caused you to recalibrate your priorities? What new paths or opportunities have emerged from it? Look to famous stories of crucible leadership involving people, such as Oprah Winfrey and Nelson Mandela, and companies, such as Chrysler and Johnson & Johnson, that have emerged from crisis stronger. They are examples of posttraumatic growth. Study and derive hope from them, and remind those connected to you to do the same.

Service.

People do better in the aftermath of trauma if they find work that benefits others—helping people close to them or their broader community or victims of events similar to the ones they have endured. Two mothers I know who'd each lost a child started a nonprofit to help bereaved families connect with others who understood their grief. Forty years later the organization thrives under the leadership of people who have faced similar losses and want to share the strength they've gained.

Another great example of service comes from Ken Falke, who was a bomb-disposal specialist in the U.S. Navy for more than 20 years. Having seen the wounds of war firsthand, he wanted to help others recover. He and his wife, Julia, began by visiting hospitalized combat veterans, but they felt that wasn't enough. So they founded the organization where I now work: the Boulder Crest Institute, which has based its Retreat for Military and Veteran Wellness programs on the posttraumatic growth model.

Of course, you don't need to start a nonprofit or a foundation to be of service. Focusing on how you can help provide relief during the continuing crisis—whether by sewing masks or producing content, stocking shelves or retraining teammates, supporting small businesses or agreeing to a temporary pay cut—can lead to growth. So can simply expressing gratitude and showing compassion and empathy to others.

How you and your group turn to service will determine whether you see the pandemic and its fallout as an unmitigated tragedy or as an opportunity to find new and better ways to live and operate. Maybe you can see how to ensure that similar emergencies are handled better in the future. Perhaps you can help those most seriously affected. Look for personal and shared missions that energize you and help you find meaning.

The Benefits

Hopefully, through this process, you and your teammates or organization will experience growth in one or more of these areas.

Personal strength.

People are often surprised by how well they have handled trauma. They are left better equipped to tackle future challenges. That can apply to teams and organizations, too. Groups often come through such trials with a clearer picture of their collective knowledge, skills, resilience, and growth potential.

Take, for example, a restaurant owner who opened up his new place this past January. By March social-distancing policies meant that his entire plan needed reconfiguring. He thought about laying off his staff, waiting for the pandemic to pass, and starting over. But he surprised himself by instead recommitting to the venture and engaging all his employees—from the kitchen and waitstaff to his business team—to see if together they could find a way to proceed.

New possibilities.

When new realities prevent the resumption of old habits, roles, and strategies, we must adapt and innovate. Leaders must have the courage and enthusiasm to test these new paths and show their people that change is to be embraced rather than feared.

The restaurant owner encouraged his group to invent a business that would draw on the resources they had—both personal and material—and allow the enterprise to survive. They began taking inventory of one another's skills and experiences and rose to the challenge of redesigning their work.

Improved relationships.

These are often born of the need to give and receive support through trying times. Trauma can help forge new relationships and make people more grateful for the ones they already have. Coming through a crisis together is a bonding experience.

This happened quickly with the restaurant employees. They began to fully appreciate the value that each one of them brought to the table. People who had hardly known one another three months earlier became closer and began functioning as a tight and flexible team.

Appreciation for life.

When confronted with fear and loss, we often become better at noticing what we still have but may have previously overlooked. Leaders can model this by acknowledging that fundamental things about living and working are to be valued. *We have a great team. Our customers appreciate the work we do. We've kept the business alive for the benefit of all who still work in it. Our organization strives toward a higher purpose.* Even something as mundane as remarking that your morning coffee tastes good counts.

Aware that most others in their industry were losing jobs, everyone at the restaurant agreed to stay on for less pay so that no one would be let go. All felt grateful to still be employed, no matter what role they might play in the revamped business. None seemed to consider any job beneath them. They appreciated having an opportunity to keep doing something worthwhile.

Spiritual growth.

This comes from reflection on the "big questions" that are often ignored in the routine of daily life. The challenges to core beliefs that we encounter in trauma often force people to become amateur theologians or philosophers to design a life worth continuing to live. Organizations, too, can be confronted with existential questions: Are we conducting our business ethically? Do we practice the principles we preach? Should we be doing something else with our valuable time and resources? What is our contribution to the betterment of society? What is the primary motive for our ongoing existence? It takes courage and foresight for leaders to open up such issues to scrutiny.

The restaurant team decided that the business should be a hybrid: part grocery store, part food prep and takeout or delivery service, and part warehouse and distribution point for donations to the local food pantry. The owner and employees wanted to serve the community and knew they would build goodwill as a by-product. They were positioning themselves for short-term survival and long-term success. Any person, team, or organization can do the same.

If you're thinking this is all too optimistic or naive, you may still be too close to the tragedy of this pandemic. That may also be true of others around you. So be patient as you work through and facilitate the process of posttraumatic growth. Those of us practicing in this field know that timing is crucial. Growth can't be forced, and it can't be rushed.

However, when you and others are ready, it is worth the effort. Let's make sure that we derive something positive from this time of struggle. The possibilities for personal and collective growth should not be squandered.

TAKEAWAYS

At some point we will be able to reflect on the long-term consequences of this terrible time. Almost certainly they will include some good along with the bad. Negative experiences can bring a recognition of personal strength, the exploration of new possibilities, improved relationships with others, a greater appreciation for life, and spiritual growth. Posttraumatic growth often happens naturally, but it can be facilitated in five ways:

- ✓ **Education.** Rethinking ourselves, our world, and our future.

- ✓ **Emotional regulation.** Managing our negative emotions and reflecting on successes and possibilities.

- ✓ **Disclosure.** Articulating what is happening and its effects.

- ✓ **Narrative development.** Shaping the story of a trauma and deriving hope from famous stories of crucible leadership.

- ✓ **Service.** Finding work that benefits others.

Adapted from "Growth After Trauma," Harvard Business Review, *July–August 2020 (product #R2004K).*

About the Contributors

URI ADONI is author of *The Unstoppable Startup: Mastering Israel's Secret Rules of Chutzpah*. He is an angel investor and venture capitalist with over 20 years of experience in the high-tech sector. He spent 12 years as a partner at Jerusalem Venture Partners Media Labs, which has listed 12 companies on NASDAQ and sold numerous others to leading tech companies such as Cisco, Microsoft, EMC, PayPal, and Sony.

JAMES BAMFORD is a senior managing director at Ankura where he serves a global client base across industries on joint venture and partnership issues. He previously founded Water Street Partners and co-led the joint venture and alliance practice at McKinsey & Company.

GERARD BAYNHAM is a senior managing director at Ankura and was previously a partner at Water Street Partners.

PETER BUCHAS is the managing director of the Quartz Efficiency Driver (QED), a software product that gives executives the data and analysis to make human capital decisions that are both quick and rigorous.

JOHN DeSARBO is a principal at ZS Associates and an expert in channel strategy and management. John manages the ZS Washington, D.C., office.

ALESSANDRO DI FIORE is the founder and CEO of the European Centre for Strategic Innovation (ECSI) and ECSI Consulting. He is based in Boston and Milan. Follow him on Twitter @alexdifiore.

DAVID ERNST is a senior managing director at Ankura where he works with clients across the globe in all phases of the joint venture life cycle from deal making to restructuring and exit. He previously founded Water Street Partners and co-led the joint venture and alliance practice at McKinsey & Company.

CLAUDIO FERNÁNDEZ-ARÁOZ is an executive fellow at Harvard Business School and the author of *It's Not the How or the What But the Who* (Harvard Business Review Press, 2014). For more than three decades, he worked at the global executive search firm Egon Zehnder where he was a partner and member of its executive committee.

MICHAEL GREINER, PhD, J.D., is an assistant professor of management for legal and ethical studies at Oakland University in Michigan. He formerly worked in business and government and as a practicing attorney.

RANJAY GULATI is the Paul R. Lawrence MBA Class of 1942 Professor of Business Administration at Harvard Business School.

STEPHEN HEIDARI-ROBINSON is the managing director of Quartz Associates (a consulting and software company that delivers organizational change), a visiting fellow at Oxford University, and coauthor of *ReOrg: How to Get It Right* (Harvard Business Review Press, 2016).

SUZANNE HEYWOOD is the chair of Quartz Associates, managing director of Exor, chair and acting CEO of CNH Industrial, and the coauthor of *ReOrg: How to Get It Right* (Harvard Business Review Press, 2016).

DANIEL ISENBERG is president of Entrepreneurship Policy Advisors and adjunct professor at Columbia Business School and Babson College. He is also the author of *Worthless, Impossible, and Stupid: How Contrarian Entrepreneurs Create and Capture Extraordinary Value* (Harvard Business Review Press, 2013).

MICHAEL G. JACOBIDES is the Sir Donald Gordon Chair of Entrepreneurship & Innovation and a professor of strategy at London Business School.

SCOTT JULIAN, PhD, is an associate professor of management at the Mike Ilitch School of Business at Wayne State University in Michigan. His research focuses on executive decision making, managerial cognition, and corporate social responsibility.

NIRMALYA KUMAR is the Lee Kong Chian Professor of Marketing at Singapore Management University and a distinguished academic fellow at INSEAD Emerging Markets Institute.

SALLY E. LORIMER is a marketing and sales consultant and a business writer for ZS Associates, a global business consulting firm. She is a coauthor of a series of sales management books, including *Sales Compensation Solutions.*

KOEN PAUWELS is the distinguished professor of marketing at Northeastern University and co-director of its Digital, Analytics, Technology, and Automation (DATA) Initiative.

MATTHIAS QIAN is an associate at Quartz and an Oxford University academic focused on machine-learning algorithms and their application to solve real-world problems.

MARTIN REEVES is the chairman of the BCG Henderson Institute in San Francisco and a coauthor of *The Imagination Machine* (forthcoming, Harvard Business Review Press).

PRABHAKANT SINHA is a cochairman of ZS Associates.

RICHARD G. TEDESCHI is a professor of psychology emeritus at the University of North Carolina at Charlotte, the distinguished chair of the Boulder Crest Institute, and a coauthor of *Posttraumatic Growth*.

MARK WIEDMAN is a senior managing director and head of international and corporate strategy at BlackRock. He is also a member of the firm's Global Executive Committee.

ANDRIS A. ZOLTNERS is a professor emeritus at Northwestern University's Kellogg School of Management. He is a cofounder of ZS Associates, a global business consulting firm, and a coauthor of a series of sales management books, including *The Power of Sales Analytics*.

Index

Is Your Business Ready for the Future?

If you enjoyed this book and want more on today's pressing business topics, turn to other books in the **Insights You Need** series from *Harvard Business Review*. Featuring HBR's latest thinking on topics critical to your company's success—from Blockchain and Cybersecurity to AI and Agile—each book will help you explore these trends and how they will impact you and your business in the future.

The most important management ideas all in one place.

We hope you enjoyed this book from *Harvard Business Review*. Now you can get even more with HBR's 10 Must Reads Boxed Set. From books on leadership and strategy to managing yourself and others, this 6-book collection delivers articles on the most essential business topics to help you succeed.

HBR's 10 Must Reads Series

The definitive collection of ideas and best practices on our most sought-after topics from the best minds in business.

- Change Management
- Collaboration
- Communication
- Emotional Intelligence
- Innovation
- Leadership
- Making Smart Decisions
- Managing Across Cultures
- Managing People
- Managing Yourself
- Strategic Marketing
- Strategy
- Teams
- The Essentials

hbr.org/mustreads

Buy for your team, clients, or event.
Visit hbr.org/bulksales for quantity discount rates.

Harvard Business Review Press